THE RESCUE OF THE DANISH JEWS
Moral Courage Under Stress

King Christian X (1870–1947), symbol of Denmark's national spirit of defiance against German encroachment on its internal affairs, calmly resumes his daily ride through Copenhagen just two days after the German aggression against Denmark on 9 April 1943. Though the many legends about the king and the Star of David are apochryphal, he was indeed a good and reliable friend of the Jews. In his quiet, unassuming yet regal manner the king elicited respect from everyone, including the enemy.

THE RESCUE OF THE DANISH JEWS

MORAL COURAGE UNDER STRESS

LEO GOLDBERGER, *Editor*

NEW YORK UNIVERSITY PRESS
New York *and* London

Manufactured in the United States of America

Library of Congress Cataloging-in-Publication Data

The Rescue of the Danish Jews.

Bibliography: p.
Includes index.
1. Jews—Denmark—History—20th century. 2. World War, 1939–1945—Jews—Rescue—Denmark. 3. Denmark—Ethnic relations. I. Goldberger, Leo.
DS135.D4R47 1987 948.9'004924 87-11253
ISBN 0-8147-3010-8
ISBN 0-8147-3011-6 (pbk.)

To Those Thousands of Danes for Whom
Heroic Acts Were Ordinary Choices

CONTENTS

ILLUSTRATIONS

FOREWORD

When World War II was terminated in so-called victory, was there any way to have faith in humanity? What are we supposed to teach our children and grandchildren about moral and ethical values as basic ingredients in forming man-to-man relationships? How shall we present to the growing generation the role of religions that were supposed to shape our faith and goodness and brotherhood at a time when we were and still are maimed in spirit by the brutality and suffering we witnessed? Shall we leave to our children the task of examining Christian culpability or the existence of God, and let them believe that there was no moral alternative to passivity toward, or cooperation with, evil? Or shall we close off our caring and not be disturbed by the passivity that diminished humanity? Many of us returned directly from the battlefields of World War II to start a normal existence. But we could not find peace of mind, and we could not concentrate only on our personal lives. Therefore, when by chance we read about the Danish rescue story, we were deeply moved. We could not believe what we read. A few documents of the rescue deeply stirred our emotions.

A pastoral letter was written by a bishop of Zealand containing a protest in the name of the church and Christianity against the atrocities of the Nazi occupation forces and their plan to annihilate the Jewish-Danish community. We have not heard or read of any official reaction to the barbarians' activities anywhere else in Europe. Representatives of governments and of religions all over the other civilized countries did not raise their voices. Is it any wonder that the Danish rescue moved us to such an extent that we decided

Dr. Elias Gechman, the founder of Tribute To The Danes in 1966, graduated from Wilno Medical School in Poland. He first escaped from the Jewish ghetto in Lwow, then from a KZ camp and spent the war years in hiding among non-Jewish friends. In 1948 he came to the United States and practiced internal medicine in New York. He died in 1973.

to see to it that the story of the Danish rescue of 1943 was made known far and wide all over the world? We wanted to prove to the world and young generations of Gentiles and Jews that there was an alternative to the passivity of the world.

Yes, we learned about isolated incidents of resistance and heroic rescue efforts by individuals and specially the famous story of the French town of Le Chambon, but in the story of the Danish rescue almost the entire nation stood up and resisted the brutal behavior of the Nazis. The idea was originally born in the mind of the late Dr. Elias Gechman to organize a tribute to the Danes, to create a source of inspiration for generations to come. The premature death of Dr. Gechman put the continuation of the organization into my hands.

Who are the people who were the only ones in the whole civilized world who resisted as a group the hangmen's massacres of innocent human beings. What is their heritage? Denmark is one of the smallest countries in Europe, with four million inhabitants and 5500 kilometers of coastline, with about 7,800 Jews including refugees who escaped Germany from 1934 to 1940. Any stratification of society was alien to the Danes. Their famous declaration that "a man is a man even if he is not bigger than a mouse" well captures their sense of basic humanity.

For the Danes, there has never been a problem of racial antagonism nor strong religious contrasts. There has never been a ghetto for Jewish countrymen. For three hundred years there has not been a serious Jewish problem.

True, an insignificant minority of self-styled Danish Nazis got infected by the anti-Semitic madness during the German occupation, but it included only the marginal members of society who were scorned by most Danes.

In 1940 Germany attacked Denmark at night, like a thief, without warning. The belief in justice and in the inner strength of humanity and freedom which formed the background of the Danish democratic way of life was shaken by that insidious attack by the Nazis. Denmark submitted out of necessity after a short period of resistance to the severe regulations imposed by the German invaders. The Danish king and the government were allowed to go on governing the internal affairs of the country, subject ultimately to German control.

In August 1943 that situation changed. An ultimatum was delivered to the Danish government calling for severe encroachments on Danish self-rule. It was found unacceptable by the Danish government, and the long-existing passive and limited active resistance to the German occupying forces changed into a warlike rebellion. The government and the king quit. They had had enough! The resistance movement in Denmark was such that Field Marshall Montgomery characterized it second to none. Factories working for Germany were blown up; railways were destroyed. Of course, these acts caused counter-terror by the Germans through imprisonment and torture.

On the night of 1 and 2 October 1943, the raid on the Danish Jews—now no longer protected by a Danish government—took place. It occurred at the time of the Jewish new year and Sabbath. Through the magnanimous German embassy official, G. F. Duckwitz, the secret plan got in the hands of several high-ranking Danish politicians, and from them to the rabbi. The day before the services for the new year started in the main synagogue, the rabbi announced that there would be no services. He warned every Jew to leave the synagogue and see to it that all Jews not present at the synagogue should be told to leave their homes and hide until a rescue to Sweden could be arranged. The Gestapo roamed through the streets, armed with lists of Jews and their addresses, breaking doors (see the film *The Only Way*), looking for their victims, but only a few were caught. The biggest and most dramatic rescue action in the history of the war was in process.

The rescue was by the unanimous will of the Danish people and had the backing of the Freedom Council, organized by the resistance leaders to coordinate efforts and communications of the many resistance groups. They accomplished the most extraordinary and heroic rescue operation of the war, hiding and transporting to safety about 7,000 Jews. The roundup was to take place during the night of 1–2 October, and two German troop ships secretly anchored in Copenhagen harbor. But on 28 September an anti-Nazi employee of the German embassy, G. F. Duckwitz, leaked the news to the leaders of the Social-Democratic party. They immediately called the leader of the Jewish community, who, by the way, did not at first believe the warning. Finally, the rabbi, who had also been told, was convinced and before the Rosh Hashanah services the news went out to every one of the Jewish faith. Relative warned relative, friend warned friend, Jew warned Jew. One ambulance driver riding through Copenhagen went through the phone book looking for people with Jewish names. He drove to their homes and offered to take them into hiding. Doctors and nurses dispersed the Jews to the hospital wards with false charts. Jews were stopped on the street and were offered keys to neighbors' apartments.

The Danish people underwent a great experience. They rose as one against the Germans and rendered active help to their innocent brethren. Some families refused to go into hiding. Those who went were transported to neutral Sweden, which let them in. There were a few Jewish groups betrayed by some fishermen and by pro-Nazi Danes. They were captured and brought to the concentration camp in Theresienstadt, which had a total of 464 Danish Jews. It was the only camp where specially grouped Jews had privileges that were ensured by the Danish king and the Red Cross.

Dr. Leon Ari Falik, president of Tribute To The Danes. He was born in eastern Galicia, studied medicine in Prague, Czechoslovakia, while enrolled at the Theological Seminary, Frankfurt, Germany. Upon graduation from both institutions, he set up medical practice in Warsaw, Poland. Escaping from Poland in September 1939 to the East, he was inducted into the Soviet army as a surgeon. At the end of the war he served as a gynecologist in two displaced-persons camps in West Berlin. Since 1948 he has practiced in the United States and is now a consulting gynecologist at the Roosevelt–St. Luke's Health Center in New York.

October 1943 was a time of triumph for the Danes. It also marked a turning point of the occupation. It marked a rebirth of hope and dignity through action. The courage of the rescuers did not come simply from their deep humanitarian commitment, from their sympathy for the persecuted, or from their hatred for the Germans. It was an idea of honor or pride shared by the entire people.

No wonder that the unique occurrence gave us hope and comfort. Coming back from Europe where the lights of freedom seemed extinguished, and everything we had loved and valued was left in ruins, the remarkable Danish rescue had proven that not the whole world was complacent and indifferent in the face of mass destruction of a people.

In order for the Danish rescue to serve as an example to be emulated, and to promote humanist ideas, we organized Tribute To The Danes. We do our work by granting scholarships to deserving young Danes, helping a number of individuals and groups to visit Israel annually, allowing them to witness the circumstances under which this biblical nation is rebuilding a modern country in spite of tremendous obstacles. Each Dane, having gotten acquainted with the reality of Israel, returns to his country and serves as a good-will ambassador, keeping a friendly contact between these two countries. In addition, our educational program promises to spread the facts of the Danish rescue over the world to children and adults by means of books dealing with the social, historical, and psychological aspects of the nation that was unique in providing us with faith in mankind.

LEON A. FALIK, M.D.
President,
Tribute To The Danes, N.Y.

EDITOR'S PREFACE

THE STORY OF how the Danes came to the aid of their Jewish population and successfully saved it from Nazi deportation is by now well known. Most have heard the legend of the Danish king who in protest and solidarity wore the Star of David. There is a variety of fanciful versions of the story, all of them untrue and yet almost impossible to eradicate from the received folklore of the Holocaust. One senses an almost pained, if not angry, resistance to attempts at demythologization.

Obviously there is a strong element of wish fulfillment at work here—as in all myths, sagas, and legends. People want the story to be true! Fortunately behind most sturdy myths a kernel of truth can be found. The story of the rescue of the Danish Jews is no exception, though I daresay that the measure of truth in this case is larger than a kernel, if allowance is made for symbolic transformations. Substitute the symbol of the king with the Danish people as a whole, and substitute further the wearing of a yellow star with the widespread and empathic compassion for the Jewish plight, and you have the truth behind the myth.

It is the true story, not the fanciful legends, that will occupy us in this volume. The factual base of the Danish rescue has found less of a place in people's memory than novelistic expressions evidently have, so it may bear repetition and detailing. The story also deserves close analytic, scholarly scrutiny. For even stripped of its romantic embellishments, the true story remains one of the few bright spots in the dark chronicles of the Holocaust. To understand and draw lessons from the historical, political, and psychosocial factors that may account for the remarkable rescue is indeed of lasting significance for mankind.

The behavior of the Danes at the most critical turning point in the war, the late summer and fall of 1943, has rightfully been recognized throughout the world as an example of moral courage under fire. Whether the Danish act is characterized as altruistic, compassionate, humanitarian, or heroic, and no matter what contextual complexities scholarly research may ascribe to it, the deed speaks for itself: almost all Jews, about 7,200 out of some 7,800,[1] were rescued from the clutches of the Nazis by a massive effort of other human beings who risked their own safety, and in some instances, their very lives. Nevertheless, it hardly needs elaborate justification to convince anyone that not only memorialization but also thorough study of the Danish act of courage is of more than passing interest.

It is the specific aim of this volume to present some thoughtful reflections on the subject of the Danish rescue. In part, these reflections grew out of the commemoration in 1983 of the fortieth anniversary of the rescue itself; in part, they evidence an ongoing interest in the rescue phenomena by Holocaust scholars, social scientists, historians, and others, each with his or her own specialized concerns. Among the several events in the United States celebrating the fortieth anniversary, Tribute To The Danes (an organization devoted exclusively to perpetuating the memory of the Danish rescue through a fellowship program), in collaboration with the American Jewish Committee, mounted a conference, entitled "Moral Choice Under Stress." A few of the papers presented at that conference (with some minor editorial modification) constitute a part but by no means all of this volume's contents.

In going beyond the framework of the conference, I have attempted to round out the topic under discussion by including some relevant background material, historical as well as anecdotal. Some of this material is presented here in English for the first time. In addition, I have chosen photos depicting Denmark during the occupation as well as some of the personalities who played a significant role in the story of the rescue. This should help bring the story home to readers.

The volume begins with a highly readable account of the rescue by the noted Norwegian American scholar Professor Samuel Abrahamsen, whose expertise lies in both Scandinavian and Judaic

Studies. Making many valuable observations, Professor Abrahamsen draws our attention to the Danish *livskunst,* a uniquely evolved "art of living" characteristic of the Danish outlook, which he finds quite relevant in trying to understand why it was specifically the large numbers of Danes who helped their fellow man. This is, in my view, an insightful point.

The noted Danish historian Professor Jørgen Hæstrup, who has tenaciously spearheaded a generation of younger historians' interest in the war period and whose own extensive volumes on all aspects of the occupation years are classics, gives us here a thorough and authoritative, yet richly textured and dramatic account. His emphasis is on the political scenario of Danish-German and Danish-Jewish relations against which the wartime experience of the Jews in Denmark must be viewed.

The reader will find a colorful close-up of the Jewish community in Denmark by the current chief rabbi of Denmark, Bent Melchior. He draws a lively, informal sketch of Danish Jewry, going back to the dawn of the century and up to the present. Rabbi Melchior's father, the late and distinguished Chief Rabbi Marcus Melchior, played an unforgettable role during the war years. Bent Melchior's piece supplements Professor Hæstrup's chapter by adding further contextual anchorage to the rescue story. Though he does not deal directly with the war period, he provides the reader with facts and figures relevant to the makeup of the Jewish community of that period. He also describes some of the strengths as well as the historic strains and tensions that inevitably characterize a small, heterogenous community.

This volume contains some quite moving accounts of the escape itself—some by prominent Danish Jews and others by well-known resistance fighters—which contain priceless gems of Danish humor and wry witticism, along with some typical Danish understatement and circumstantial embellishments. I am especially pleased to have the specially prepared contribution by the celebrated director, actor, and author of many fine autobiographical Danish novels Sam Besekow. His bittersweet descriptions and Chagall-like flights of fancy in the midst of his personal "pogrom" experience are unforgettably poignant.

As editor, I have taken the liberty of including a brief narrative of my own experience as a youngster caught in the maelstrom of occupied Denmark when my family and I were among the lucky ones to survive the Holocaust in Europe. Needless to say, it left a lasting impression along with a deep sense of gratitude toward the Danes. In the nature of an epilogue, I have also included an overview of the factors that seem to me most relevant to a full appreciation of the event of the Danish rescue.

For the record, it should be noted that the conference, "Moral Choice Under Stress," was preceded by a festive luncheon with many guests representing governmental and diplomatic officialdom, plus well-wishing messages from President Ronald Reagan and Governor Mario Cuomo of New York State. The conference took place at the Sutton Place Synagogue in New York on 23 October 1983, with the distinguished Rabbi Marc Tanenbaum of the American Jewish Committee serving as moderator. His splendid introduction to the conference will be found in chapter 9. Finally, and again for the historic record, I want to mention, with appropriate filial pride, the very moving rendition of *Modim* (a hymn of thankfulness) offered by my father, Cantor Eugene Goldberger, at the festivities. My father, who had for more than a decade served as a cantor in the Copenhagen synagogue, was in the middle of *slichot* services on that fateful morning, 29 September 1943, when Rabbi Marcus Melchior interrupted the solemn proceedings to relay the warning of the imminent action against the Jews. His *Modim,* I know, was truly from the heart.

NOTE

1. The reader should note that the statistical information concerning the number of Jews living in Denmark during the war, the number who succeeded in fleeing to Sweden, and the number caught and deported to Theresienstadt tends to vary somewhat in the Holocaust literature. In part, this is due to the tendency of many authors to approximate using different round numbers. The inconsistent figures may also be due to the fact that some authors include half-Jews in their count while others do not. Whether or not the count includes about 150 Jews who had left Denmark between 1940 and 1943 is yet another variable. For the reader's orientation, the basic numerical facts appear to be these: At the critical juncture, October 1943, a total of some 6,450–6,500 Jews lived in Denmark (about 1,500 of whom were refugees who had come after 1933). If one adds the 1,300 offspring of

mixed marriages (i.e., half-Jews), the total number reaches a maximum of 7800. A total of 7,220 of these succeeded in escaping to Sweden (accompanied by 686 non-Jewish spouses out of a total of 936 mixed marriages). There were thus some 580 who failed to escape, 464 of whom were held in Theresienstadt KZ camp until April 1945, when the 425 who survived the camp (plus a few who were born in the camp) were transferred by the Red Cross to Sweden. Of those unaccounted for, some remained hidden or had special permission to stay, while another relatively small group were the victims of accidental drowning or chose to commit suicide rather than face German captivity.

REFERENCES

Margolinsky, Julius. *Statististke Undersøgelser over Alders og Kønsfordeling blandt Flygtninge fra Danmark i Sverige*. Stockholm, 1945. Mimeographed.

Yahil, Leni. *The Rescue of Danish Jewry: Test of a Democracy*. Philadelphia: Jewish Publication Society of America, 1969.

ACKNOWLEDGMENTS

THIS PROJECT WAS inspired and underwritten by Tribute To The Danes, a New York–based organization founded in 1966 to make known the exemplary Danish rescue of their Jewish brethren. Grateful acknowledgment is made to its indefatigable president, Dr. Leon Arie Falik, and to his wife, Dr. Ruth F. Lax, the codirector of research. Members of the board who played a significant role as advisors and supporters should also be mentioned: Dr. Marion Oliner, Henry Winestine, Dr. Joan Shapiro, Dr. Jehuda Nir, and Dr. Marvin Kristein. Bernice Wolf Gordon and Dr. Milan Stroeger, both now deceased, are also remembered for their valuable input.

Among those who played a key role in helping Dr. Falik organize the conference "Moral Choice Under Stress," which was jointly sponsored by Tribute To The Danes and the American Jewish Committee and out of which this project grew, mention should be made of Ann Roiphe, Rabbi Tanenbaum, David Geller, Judith Benke, and Frank Brecker.

Several Danish friends were exceedingly helpful and generous with their time and effort. The Danish architect Salli Besiakov, my friendship with whom goes back to 1943 when we were both students in the Danish refugee school in Gothenburg, Sweden, served as my go-between and right-hand man in Copenhagen. To him goes the credit for drawing the map of Denmark for this volume, an exacting task that he met with his characteristic aplomb and good humor. The tough job of providing a translation from Danish to English of some of the chapters in this volume fell in part on the shoulders of Nina Juel (who made a preliminary draft of Jørgen Hæstrup's and Bent Melchior's articles) and more heavily on Ida Pagh, who did the work on Valdemar Koppel's and Sam Besekow's pieces as a labor of love and under tremendous time pressure.

Others in Denmark who deserve mention are Mogens Staffeldt, Fini Schulsinger, Simo Køppe, Ulf Haxen, Jørgen Barfoed, Rosa Krotoschinsky, Nils Koppel, Bent Rosenbaum and Leif Rosenstock who were helpful in a variety of ways during my several recent visits to Denmark.

I owe an enormous debt to my wife, Dr. Nancy R. Goldberger, for her tireless help on the word processor and off. She introduced numerous stylistic improvements and provided supportive feedback.

Kitty Moore, senior editor at New York University Press, was her usual creative self, giving freely of her expertise and warm encouragement. She knows how grateful I am.

Finally, my thanks to the contributors who allowed free use of their writings and to the publishers who granted permission to reproduce materials.

The following organizations and individuals are gratefully acknowledged for permission to use the photographs in this volume:

Museum of Denmark's Fight for Freedom, 1940–1945, Copenhagen
Nordisk Presse Foto, Copenhagen
Politikens Presse Foto, Copenhagen
Fyns Presse Foto, Copenhagen
The Royal Library, Copenhagen
Sam Besekow
Salli Besiakov
Leon A. Falik
Nils Koppel

CONTRIBUTORS

SAMUEL ABRAHAMSEN, Ph.D. Founder and former chairman, Department of Judaic Studies, Brooklyn College; cochair, Seminar of Scandinavian Studies, CUNY Graduate Center. He has held key positions in the American Jewish Congress and the American Scandinavian Foundation and is the recipient of many honors. His most recent publication is *The Holocaust in Norway in Historical Perspective* (Holocaust Publications, 1987).

SAM BESEKOW. Danish theater personality and author. For more than half a century Sam Besekow has been a household name in Danish theater, radio, and, in more recent years, television, as director, actor, and storyteller. He has served the prestigious Royal Danish Theatre as director of plays by Strindberg, Chekhov, O'Neill, Anouilh, Beckett, and Albee, among others. Of more than a dozen books, perhaps his most celebrated is *Skræd-derens Søn* ([*The Tailor's Son*], Borgen, 1964).

ARTHUR A. COHEN. Author, editor, and publisher. Recently deceased, he was one of the most distinguished and brilliant thinkers on the American Jewish scene and had been a Fellow of Jewish Philosophy, Jewish Theological Seminary of America. His books include *The Tremendum: A Theological Interpretation of the Holocaust* (Crossroads, 1981) and a novel based on the life of Hannah Arendt, entitled *An Admirable Woman* (Godine, 1983).

LEON A. FALIK, M.D. President of Tribute To The Danes. Born in Poland, he survived the Holocaust by serving as a surgeon in the Russian army. For many years deeply devoted to Tribute To The Danes, he took over the organization's leadership upon the death of its founder, Dr. Elias Gechman.

LEO GOLDBERGER, Ph.D. Professor of psychology, New York University. Currently editor in chief of the quarterly interdisciplinary journal *Psychoanalysis & Contemporary Thought* (International Universities Press), he was coeditor of *Handbook of Stress* (Free Press, 1982) and has done extensive research on styles of human adaptation. He is vice-president of Tribute To The Danes, and is on the board of the Anti-Defamation League of B'nai Brith's International Center for Holocaust Studies.

JØRGEN HÆSTRUP, Ph.D. Danish historian, Odense University. The doyen of researchers on the Danish war years and the resistance movement. Among his books in English are *Secret Alliance* (New York University Press, 1985) and *Passage to Palestine* (Odense University Press, 1983). In 1977 he was awarded the Royal Danish Scientific Society's gold medal.

OTTO F. KERNBERG, M.D. Professor of psychiatry, Cornell University Medical College; faculty, Columbia University Center for Psychoanalytic Training and Research. A prolific writer on psychoanalytic subjects, notably narcissism and its treatment, object relations, and group process, his most recent book is *Severe Personality Disorders* (Yale University Press, 1984).

JØRGEN KIELER, M.D., D.Sc. Director, The Danish Cancer Society. He was a leading member of the Danish resistance movement. (He worked on the illegal paper *Frit Danmark* and later engaged in active sabotage as a member of the Holger Danske group.) For many years he has been the president of the Freedom Foundation in Denmark, which provides support to Danish concentration camp victims.

VALDEMAR KOPPEL. Distinguished Danish journalist and editor. He was the editor in chief of *Politiken,* a leading Danish daily newspaper. He died in 1949.

BENT MELCHIOR. Chief rabbi of Denmark. Served as a volunteer in the Hagana, 1948–1949. Since his ordination in London in 1963 he has served the Jewish community in Denmark and became chief rabbi in 1970. He lectures on Jewish literature at the University of Copenhagen and is the author of several books on Judaic subjects, including *Jødedommen; En Tekstcollage* ([*Judaism: A Textual Col-*

lage], Gyldendal, 1977). Among his many organizational involvements Rabbi Melchior is chairman of the Tribute To The Danes' Scholarship Selection Committee in Denmark.

HERBERT PUNDIK. Prominent Danish journalist. Since 1970, he has been editor in chief of *Politiken,* one of the leading newspapers in Denmark. He was a volunteer in the Danish Brigade in Sweden in 1945 and served in the Hagana in 1948–1949. Between 1956 and 1969 he was the foreign correspondent to Danish radio from Israel, and he has been the recipient of the Cavling prize—the highest award for journalistic excellence. Among his books are *Israel og Naboerne* ([*Israel and Her Neighbors*], Munksgaard, 1982).

JAROSLAV PELIKAN, Ph.D. Religious historian. He is Sterling Professor of History at Yale University and an ordained minister in the Lutheran Church. He is the author of numerous books, among them *From Luther to Kierkegaard* (Concordia, 1950), *The Riddle of Roman Catholicism* (Abingdon, 1959), the multivolumed *The Christian Tradition* (University of Chicago Press, 1971), and *The Vindication of Tradition* (Yale University Press, 1984). He is the editor of a thirty-volume edition of Martin Luther's *Works* (Concordia, 1959–1961). In 1983 he was given the singular honor of delivering the Thomas Jefferson Lecture of the National Endowment for the Humanities.

MARC H. TANENBAUM. Rabbi; director of interreligious affairs, American Jewish Committee since 1961. Rabbi Tanenbaum is perhaps one of the most visible Jewish spokesmen in the United States—writer, editor, television panelist, White House conferee, and member of the National Council of Christians and Jews. Between 1954 and 1960, he served as executive director of the Synagogue Council of America. He is the author of *Religious Values in an Age of Violence* (The Pere Marquette Theological Lecture, Marquette, 1976) and coeditor of *Evangelicals and Jews* (Baker Books, 1978).

INTRODUCTION AND HISTORICAL BACKGROUND

A boatload of Danish Jews on their way to Sweden. All along the coastline Jews made their escape in a variety of boats, large and small, with the help of thousands of Danes, many with no previous experience in illegal resistance activity. At great risk, the Danes opened their doors to Jews who needed a place to hide before arrangements with a skipper were finalized or where they could wait until the coast was clear of German patrol boats. They helped locate old and indigent Jews, moving them to hospitals before arranging their escape across the sound. They helped gather the money needed to finance the escape. During the first two weeks of October 1943 more than 90 percent of the jews living in Denmark were miraculously ferried to safety in Sweden. There were of course some tragedies and mishaps—a few committed suicide, others drowned, some were caught in flight, while still others were caught in their homes on the night of the roundup. All told, only 464 Jews from Denmark ended up in Theresienstadt concentration camp, and most of these were ultimately saved as well.

1.

THE RESCUE OF DENMARK'S JEWS[1]

SAMUEL ABRAHAMSEN

ON THE MORNING of the Jewish New Year (Rosh Hashanah), 29 September 1943, the acting chief rabbi of Denmark, Marcus Melchior, hurriedly entered the Great Synagogue in Krystalgade in Copenhagen. During the divine service he announced to the stunned congregation that a German action to arrest and deport all Jews would start that night.[1] "You must leave immediately, warn all your friends and relatives and go into hiding," the rabbi said. This was easier said than done. Where to hide, where to flee, where to find friends on a few hours' notice? Would the Nazi scheme to annihilate the total European Jewish population also succeed in destroying the oldest Scandinavian Jewish community, dating back to 1622?

The fact is, however, that more than 95 percent of the Danish Jews were rescued. This rescue constituted one of the most courageous and dramatic episodes during World War II; the diabolic Nazi scheme to exterminate innocent people in the occupied countries was averted in Denmark. Overnight the Nazi tyranny was confronted with thousands of Danes determined to thwart any effort to exterminate their Jewish fellowmen.

When Germany invaded Denmark in the early hours of 9 April 1940, Denmark offered only token resistance and was rewarded with a degree of autonomy unheard of in a territory under German

Reprinted from *The American Scandinavian Review*, vol. 60, no. 2 (June 1972) (by permission).

domination. Denmark's unique position as a "model protectorate" meant it could retain its own government, foreign office, and armed forces. Far from controlling the internal and external affairs of Denmark, Germany pledged no interference in Denmark's political independence. The constitutional protection of the Bill of Rights, including the lives and rights of Denmark's Jews, was to be scrupulously upheld.

This mutual agreement became the foundation for a Danish-German *modus operandi* which lasted for about three and a half years. By the fall of 1943 the German armies were in retreat from El Alamein in North Africa to Stalingrad. The Danish resistance movement had by this time increased in militancy. During the month of August sabotage against German installations had reached its peak, ending in general strikes by the Danes. The Germans reacted violently by introducing a curfew, the seizing of hostages, and establishing a reign of terror. On 28 August 1943, the Danish government was presented with an ultimatum whereby the German occupying power declared martial law throughout Denmark, the death penalty for sabotage, a total ban on strikes and demonstrations, and a complete censorship of the press.[2] The Danish government rejected these demands with impunity; this led to a German declaration of a state of emergency, internment of the Danish army, and persecution of Danish Jews. The deportations were to be carried out during the night of the Jewish new year, 1-2 October 1943, when the Jews would be at home.

Contrary to their own propaganda the Nazis had to admit, after a survey was taken in 1943, that the small Danish Jewish population played no significant role either politically or economically. Their own research before deciding upon anti-Jewish measures had proven that the Danes would not permit anti-Semitism, a tradition going back to the year 1690 when a Danish police commissioner was removed for having suggested the establishment of a Jewish ghetto in Copenhagen. But Nazi Germany still went ahead with its plans of deportation which proved that the Nazi genocide of Jews was irrevocable, "no matter how big the cost, not matter how small the yield."[3] With the start of Jewish persecutions the Danish resistance movement entered upon a new chapter.

In restrospect it seems almost incredible that peace-loving and easy-going Danes would change overnight from law-abiding citizens to become underground fighters, who would live under false names and addresses, constantly moving from one hiding place to another and using false identification cards to risk their lives to save their fellow Danes. Ever since 1942, however, many "cells," "study groups," "book circles," or "sewing clubs" had been systematically organized throughout Denmark. In order to create effective, illegal organizations they were established along professional lines, such as clergymen, doctors, engineers, professors, trade union members, civil servants, etc. The twin objectives of these cells were to increase illegal resistance against the occupying power, and to provide close contact with the Allies and the Free Danish Forces abroad, especially in London. Here the freedom fighter Christmas Møller had established his headquarters in 1942. When the legal Danish government resigned in August 1943, a remarkable governing body known as the underground Freedom Council came into existence led by such outstanding figures as Frode Jakobsen, Mogens Fog, Arne Sørensen, and many other patriots. Filling a political vacuum, the Freedom Council soon became the *de facto* government and the major instrumental for organizing resistance to Nazi terrorism and escape from deportation.

All groups participated in the rescue of the Jews. One of them, the Danish physicians, assisted more than two thousand Jews. On one day, 7 October 1943, 140 Jews who had been in hiding all over Copenhagen were brought to Bispebjerg Hospital and given refuge in the psychiatric ward or in the nurses' residences. From here the Jews were transported in ambulances, sanitation trucks, or fire engines to fishing boats or other small vessels which ferried the refugees over to Sweden. The Danish physicians quickly became known as "Den Hvide Brigade" (the White Brigade), who in addition to fighting general human illnesses also fought effectively against the disease of anti-Semitism.

It was this coordinated action by countless fishermen, farmers, businessmen, and taxi and ambulance drivers who together with the organized members of the Freedom Council played a decisive role in the successful rescue of Danish Jewry. Out of a total Jewish population of 7,800 (including 1,300 half Jews) about 7,200 were transported to Sweden. It was a perilous voyage; the weather was rough, and minefields and German patrol boats had to be avoided.

This rescue in October 1943, known as "Little Dunkirk," was a totally spontaneous action; without spontaneity the escape could not possibly have succeeded. Neither could the transport of so many human beings have been achieved without proper organization. This apparent paradox between spontaneous versus organized action may best be understood through the actions and attitudes of the church and the University of Copenhagen. These two institutions were in the forefront of mobilizing public protests against the Nazis. The clergy had about 90 percent of its membership participating in the underground, the university close to 100 percent.

On 2 October 1943, the faculty and students at the University of Copenhagen decided to suspend all classes "in view of the disasters which have overtaken our fellow citizens." Most Jews had by this time gone into hiding but one of the major difficulties was how to locate them. They couldn't remain safely in hiding for more than a few days at the most, and in order to reach Sweden immediate assistance was clearly needed. For these purposes the students used two of their clubs, Akademisk Skytteforenings Terrain-sportsafdeling (the Academic Rifle- and Cross-country Sports Club) to comb the forests, and bring the Jews to fishing boats through an elaborate route maintained by Studenternes Efterretnings-tjeneste (Students' Intelligence Service). Both of these organizations had been established long before the German invasion.

The Danish church had, on 29 September 1943, sent a protest against Jewish persecutions to the Nazi authorities. The protest was distributed by all the bishops of Denmark. It was read from the pulpits in the Danish churches on Sunday, 3 October 1943, and said in part:

> Wherever Jews are persecuted because of their religion or race it is the duty of the Christian Church to protest against such persecution, because it is in conflict with the sense of justice inherent in the Danish people and inseparable from our Danish Christian culture through centuries. True to this spirit and according to the text of the Act of the Constitution all Danish citizens enjoy equal rights and responsibilities before the Law and full religious freedom. We understand religious freedom as the right to exercise our worship of God as our vocation and conscience bid us and in such a manner that race and religion per se can never justify that a person be deprived of his rights, freedom or property. Our different religious views notwithstanding, we shall fight for the cause that our Jewish

> brothers and sisters may preserve the same freedom which we ourselves evaluate more highly than life itself. With the leaders of the Danish Church there is a clear understanding of our duty to be law-abiding citizens who will not groundlessly rebel against the authorities, but at the same time our conscience bids us to assert the Law and protest against any violation of the Law. We shall therefore in any given event unequivocally adhere to the concept that we must obey God before we obey man.[4]

This declaration was personally signed by Copenhagen's bishop, H. Fuglsang Damgaard on behalf of Denmark's bishops.

This courageous statement by the Danish Church expressed the democratic principle of personal responsibility as opposed to the Nazi ideology of committing murder because Hitler had so ordered. The actions by the church, the students, and faculties of the universities demonstrated that the intellectual elite of Denmark was engaged in a deadly battle to maintain the ethical and moral values of the nation. In the end this battle turned in favor of the Danes. Although detailed plans had been made for deportation and complete annihilation of all Danish Jews, this disaster did not at all reach the dimensions planned by the Nazis. True, Denmark did become *Judenrein* (clean of Jews) during the month of October 1943, not as a result of the Nazi ideology but as a result of the Danish effort to assist and save human beings. Little did Hitler and Eichmann realize how quickly the Danish Jews would in fact disappear to make the country "clean of Jews." It seems like the talmudic saying that "the one who rescues one single human being is regarded as having saved all humanity" had become part of Danish culture. The Danes went forth during World War II to do deeds in civic responsibility unparalleled in the history of the Holocaust. While most of the rest of the world was a silent witness to the genocide of six million innocent people, the Danes not only protested verbally and in writing, but at great personal risk rescued thousands of the condemned Jews. The statement that the Holocaust was inevitable in all occupied countries is simply not true.

The question is rather: why was the rescue of so many Jews successful to such an extent in Denmark, but nowhere else? Many explanations have been offered: the time factor, proximity to neutral Sweden, the small size of the Jewish population, or the crucial role played by the German naval attaché, Georg Ferdinand Duckwitz, who revealed the secret plans to the late Prime Minister Hans Hedtoft, one of the main leaders of the Danish resistance movement. All these factors must, of course, be taken into account, but they overlook some basic characteristics of the Danes and Danish society. This nation had developed over the centuries what the Danes call *livskunst,* (the art of living). It was a society where people *cared* about one another, where respect for individual and religious differences, self-reliance, cooperation, and good humor had become hallmarks of a civilized nation. These moral, intellectual, and ethical attitudes made the Danes say: "The Jews are our fellow citizens and fellow human beings; we shall not give them up for slaughter." And they did not. That's why the Danes became the *real* victors in Europe. They did not lose their souls.

The diabolic plan to exterminate innocent Jews so outraged the Danish population that it *united* the nation against the Nazis and established a popular basis for the Danish resistance movement. From then on to the very end of the war, in May 1945, the masses of the population were drawn into an unyielding fight against the German occupiers. The large-scale Jewish persecutions, which failed, gave rise to a popular uprising based on illegal organizations bent on helping to destroy the Nazi war machine and to save the total Jewish population from certain annihilation.

But not all the Danish Jews were saved, four hundred and sixty-four women, children, and men, were rounded up, arrested, and deported to the Theresienstadt concentration camp. Some were caught while in hiding, among them sixty at the Gilleleje Church, betrayed by an informer;[5] some committed suicide rather than face deportation and death; others were too old or too poor, without means or connections to facilitate their own rescue. Some even refused to leave altogether, preferring to retain the illusion that "it can't happen to us."

In this connection it is important to recall the psychological conditioning that had taken place during the three and a half years of German occupation. The Jewish community leaders in Denmark had from the beginning of the occupation carefully abstained from any illegal action in order not to provoke the Nazi authorities. Even planning for escape or planning to go into hiding was frowned upon, especially after 15 March 1943, when fifteen young Danish Jews succeeded in escaping to Sweden. Six escaped while hiding in freight trains, and nine crossed in fishing vessels from Bornholm to Sweden, where the Swedish press acclaimed this act as a courageous achievement. But in Denmark the Danish police under German pressure warned "all Jewish organizations against lending a hand to such ventures and threatened all young Jews with internment."[6]

Since all Danish Jews had been protected by humane laws and regulations for over a century and a quarter, the Jewish community leaders felt safe in relying upon obedience to Danish laws as the only alternative for survival, especially if "minor adjustments," such as suspension of freedom of the press and assembly for Jews, had to be made, in the erroneous belief that these acts would avert the Nazi wrath. The Danish authorities supported this assumption which led to the suspension already in April 1940, of the Jewish official publication *Jødisk Familieblad* (*Jewish Family Journal*) as well as the suspension of all lectures on Jewish topics to the general public. Although objective treatment of Judaism in books or articles was seldom to appear during the occupation, it is interesting to note that a book entitled *Glimpses of Judaism* was written by two Copenhagen rabbis, Marcus Melchior and W. S. Jacobson. A copy of the book was sent to His Majesty King Christian X who on many occasions had expressed his sympathy for the Jewish people and their special problems. It is a fact that the king in April 1933, the same year that Hitler came to power in Germany, was the guest of honor of the Jewish community in its synagogue, which celebrated its centenary.

On New Year's Day 1942, Rabbi Melchior received a letter in the king's own handwriting reaffirming his warm and active support of Jews during the German occupation. Another act of personal courage took place in the Theresienstadt concentration camp. In contrast to the treatment of Jews in other European countries the Danish Jews were never abandoned by their countrymen. The Danes actively protested the deportations; they sent valuable food parcels through the Danish Red Cross; they worked tirelessly to prevent Danish Jews from being transferred from Theresienstadt to the death camp in Auschwitz; and last, but not least, the Danes succeeded by constant pressure in obtaining permission from the Nazi authorities to send a delegation of inspection to Theresienstadt. When the visiting delegation arrived on 24 June 1944, Chief Rabbi M. Friediger from Copenhagen received personal messages and greetings from Bishop Fuglsang Damgaard and the king,[7] who at this time was himself a German prisoner under house arrest. These humane acts were an inspiration to freedom fighters all over the world.

Before the vast majority of Danish Jews were ferried across to Sweden, that country, on 2 October 1943, issued a proclamation welcoming all Danish refugees. A similar statement in 1942 from Sweden to Germany offering asylum to the persecuted Norwegian Jews had been rejected by the Nazis as undue interference in domestic affairs. The small Jewish communities in Norway suffered severe losses of nearly half of their members.[8] In October 1943, Denmark had to place its faith in Sweden to open its borders to Danish refugees; this came about by mobilizing Swedish public opinion to participate in the illegal rescue of the Jews. The Danish Freedom Council had debated intensively what to do with thousands of Jews in hiding. They needed a safe place to go. Here again there were many examples of personal intervention, notably that of the nuclear scientist Niels Bohr. He had escaped to Sweden in September 1943, and had started immediate negotiations with the Swedish Foreign Minister Christian Günther and Under Secretary Erik Boheman. These negotiations didn't seem to lead to the desired result, and accordingly Dr. Bohr asked for an audience with King Gustaf V on the same evening as the first persecutions of Denmark's Jews took place.[9] The upshot was that the Swedish radio and press announced to a startled world that all Danish Jews would be welcome. They now had a sanctuary to which they could escape.

Twenty-five years later inspiring ceremonies took place simultaneously in Jerusalem and Copenhagen to commemorate these events. In Copenhagen the name of Grønttorvet (the Vegetable Market Place) was changed to *Israel Square.* And the *Beth Hakerem Park* in Jerusalem was renamed Kikar Daniah (Denmark Square). In the presence of the Danish Minister of Welfare, Mrs. Nathalie Lind; Mayor of Jerusalem Teddy Kollek, and the Danish sculptor Harald Isenstein, a model of a Danish fishing boat and a plaque were unveiled. The inscription on the plaque reads in English:

> In October 1943 the Danish people and the resistance movement defied Nazi occupation of their country to rescue their fellow citizens. During ten nights, almost all Danish Jewry, over 7,000 people, were spirited across the Øresund in fishing boats and other

> small craft to safety in Sweden. Danish courage and Swedish generosity gave indelible proof of human values in time of barbarism. Israel and Jews all over the world will never forget.[10]

And true to this noble sentiment the saga of the rescue of the Danish Jews will remain an eternal light in a world of spiritual darkness. The Jews found upon their return to Denmark that friends and neighbors had tended their gardens, taken care of their homes and businesses. On returning they were met with a warm welcome.

A noted Danish historian of Jewish affairs Julius Margolinsky, assessed the dramatic events of October 1943 by drawing attention to the biblical story of Esther who had saved the Persian Jews from Haman's wrath more than twenty-five hundred years ago. If the Bible had not already been concluded it would have been possible that the "story about October 1943, might have been included in the Holy Scriptures as an eternal reminder for succeeding generations."[11]

NOTES

1. Marcus Melchior, *A Rabbi Remembers,* (New York: Lyle Stuart, 1968), p. 179.
2. Leni Yahil, *The Rescue of Danish Jewry: Test of a Democracy.* (Philadelphia: Jewish Publication Society of America, 1969), p. 124.
3. Raul Hilberg, *The Destruction of the European Jews,* (New York: Quadrangle, 1967) p. 355.
4. Harald Sandbæck and N. J. Rald, (eds.), *Den Danske Kirke under Besættelsen,* Copenhagen: H. Hirschsprung Forlag, 1945), pp. 21–22.
5. Harold Flender, *Rescue in Denmark* (New York: Simon & Schuster, 1963), p. 211. Whether this in fact was so was not fully established in the Danish courts; see C. Tortzen. *Gilleleje October 1943.* Copenhagen: Fremad, 1970, p. 60.
6. S. Adler-Rudel, "A Chronicle of Rescue Efforts," *Yearbook of the Leo Baeck Institute of Jews from Germany,* vol. 9 (London: Secker and Warburg, 1966) p. 224.
7. Max Friediger, *Theresienstadt* (Copenhagen: J. Fr. Clausen's Forlag 1946), p. 111. (Dr. Friediger, who had been arrested on 29 August 1943 and detained in Horserød camp, was deported to Theresienstadt along with those captured in the early days and weeks in October and November.)
8. Hugo Valentin, "Rescue and Relief Activities in behalf of Jewish Victims of Nazism in Scandinavia," *YIVO Annual of Jewish Social Science,* vol. 8 (New York: Yiddish Scientific Institute, 1953), p. 234.
9. *Doc. 0-27/13,* p. 15, 17 July 1958, at Yad Vashem.
10. This inscription is also in Hebrew and in Swedish.
11. Aage Bertelsen, *Oktober 1943* New York: Putnam, 1954).

Map of Denmark. (Courtesy of Salli Besiakov).

2.

THE DANISH JEWS AND THE GERMAN OCCUPATION

JØRGEN HÆSTRUP

JEWISH REACTIONS TO THE OCCUPATION OF DENMARK

I STILL REMEMBER that I was able to sleep that night. Even today, I am still astonished when I think of it."[1] Those were the words used by C. B. Henriques, the chairman of the Danish Jewish Community in 1943, in describing the fatal night between 28 and 29 September 1943. In the evening of the twenty-eighth, notwithstanding the darkness and curfew, Henriques was visited by Hans Hedtoft, H. C. Hansen, and Herman Dedichen, [all prominent Danish politicians]. The aim of their visit was to deliver the ominous message that a German "action" against the Danish Jews was imminent. In fact, it was only three days away.

Known for his strong personality, Henriques had led the Jewish community through three years of German occupation with his customary, almost cold-blooded toughness. Nevertheless, in hindsight, one cannot help but feel amazement, if not admiration, for the serenity he appears to have maintained—especially when one

First published in Harold Jørgensen, ed., *Indenfor Murene: Jødisk liv i Danmark 1684–1984* (Copenhagen: Selskabet for dansk jødisk Historie, C. A. Reitzels Forlag, 1984). Reprinted by permission of the author. Translated by Leo Goldberger. Editor's interpolations appear in brackets and in Notes.

considers that the warning took him by complete surprise. Only a few hours earlier he had been assured by the Danish foreign ministry and by the Danish bishop Fuglsang Damgaard that rumors of an impending action were just that, rumors. What he obviously did not know was that these reassurances were based on an identical source—the deceptive German reich plentipotentiary in Denmark, Werner Best. Henriques's immediate response to Hans Hedtoft was to exclaim, "You are lying!" Not until his visitors indicated that their information was based on a most reliable source—namely, the German shipping attaché [and close friend of Best], Georg F. Duckwitz, did Henriques surrrender to the facts.

Was his ability to sleep that night evidence of his particular strength or of Jewish fatalism, and to what extent was this characteristic shared by his fellow Jews on that night and during the 1,267 nights since the German occupation began on 9 April 1940? There was, on that night in 1943, at least one thing that Henriques could not possibly have anticipated, namely the events that were to take place in the subsequent weeks across the Øresund and Kattegat [bodies of water separating Denmark and Sweden].

To understand the events that took place in 1943 one needs to go back to 1940 and determine the reaction of the Jewish community—native Danish Jews as well as refugees—to the German invasion and how it responded to the stress each and every Jew in Denmark must have experienced.

In general, the sudden and unexpected invasion welded a common fate shared by everyone living within the Danish borders on the ninth of April. Jews in Denmark were affected, as were all Danish citizens, by the conditions and gradual unfolding of the occupation. Though, of course, the Jews in Denmark were a particularly vulnerable group, their fate was linked to the Danish fate and dependent upon Danish politics. Despite the presence of strong Jewish emotions and fears, the occupation, by and large, was experienced not merely as a Jewish, but also as a Danish misfortune. Dr. Marcus Melchior [then the "second" rabbi, who became the Danish chief rabbi in 1947] expressed it in these words:

> Of course I was as scared, as horrified, as much in despair as everybody else. I was not only Danish, I was Jewish. What was

Georg Ferdinand Duckwitz (1904–1973), the courageous German who tried to intercept Dr. Best's telegram and then finally blew the whistle on the planned action of 1–2 October 1943, giving the Jews at least three days' warning. Duckwitz, who quite early was disenchanted with the Nazi party, had worked in Denmark from 1928 to 1933 and again from 1939 on as a shipping expert in the German embassy. Because he was Dr. Best's confidant and because he had good connections among Danish political leaders he is credited with mediating and muting the impact of the German occupation at several critical junctures. After the war he served as West Germany's ambassador to Denmark from 1955 to 1958.

Hans Hedtoft (1903–1955), one of the Danish political leaders who on 28 September 1943 was alerted by Duckwitz of the impending roundup of the Jews. Hans Hedtoft, who shortly after the war became Denmark's prime minister, was known for his staunch antifascist stance within the Social-Democratic party. The Germans demanded his removal from political office as early as February 1941.

C. B. Henriques (1870–1957, left), the highly respected supreme-court barrister and long-time head of the Danish Jewish community, who steered the fate of the Jews by insisting that they place their trust in the Danish king and government. His reaction to Hans Hedtoft's urgent message from Duckwitz late on 28 September was stunned disbelief as he had just been reassured by Niels Svenningsen—the highest-ranking Danish official still functioning—that Dr. Best denied any knowledge of a planned action against the Jews. Svenningsen, the bishop of Copenhagen, and even the king himself had conveyed their warning to Dr. Best: the persecution of Jews was totally unacceptable and would have dire consequences for Danish-German relations. When the Jewish action took place anyway, a resounding protest ensued across the land.

going to happen to "us" now? But regardless of this special fear, the predominant emotion in me, as in Danish Jews in general on this April 9th, was this: What about Denmark? What about our small, decent, delicate, gentle, quietly happy fatherland? What about the King? . . . We turned to the day's tasks stunned and dulled, but compelled to pretend that the world was still standing.[2]

Melchior also mentioned his casual meeting with C. B. Henriques in the morning of 9 April, quoting Henriques's first words when receiving the message of the German invasion, namely, "They are taking our lovely country."

The searching questions Melchior was asking, about the day that lay ahead and the future in general, could have been asked by every Dane. Everyone was asking questions and no one had the answer. The inharmonious sound of unanswered questions dominated that day.

The occupation struck the country with paralysing suddenness. From one day to the next the population was faced with a *fait accompli*. The intelligence warnings received during the first days of April were not common knowledge to the general public at the time. In looking back to the first days and weeks of the German occupation, the knowledge one has today should, of course, not be confounded with what one knew at the time. The first reaction was shock followed by a deep sense of uncertainty. Nobody could forecast what the future held for Denmark under German occupation nor predict whether the German military adventure in Norway might not lead to the fall of Germany. The Allies had not yet taken any action. Would they—and would they be able to—intervene and put an end to the spreading invasion of Nazism? Shock as well as uncertainty precluded action. For the Jews in Denmark, as for everybody else, there was no course other than to continue the daily routine and, to the extent possible, carry on as if it were a normal day. Indeed, this is what happened and what had to happen. Only gradually did people realize that the occupation—despite the misfortune and costs it implied for the country—did not have any immediate consequences for the individual citizen, not even for most of the Jewish refugees [Jews without Danish citizenship] living in Denmark on 9 April 1940. This lack of direct impact on individuals soon became a Danish realization and a

A few Danes grimly watch a passing parade of Germans on the streets of Copenhagen. Except for scattered incidents of active sabotage and the beginning of an extremely significant underground press (growing steadily to more than five-hundred separate papers and three-hundred books and pamphlets), organized resistance took a few years to move into high gear. But antipathy and smoldering resentment toward the unwelcome guests was widespread from the start. Any form of fraternization with the Germans was viewed with scorn.

Jewish one as well, and forms the background against which one can understand the perspective of the Jewish community.

How many native Danish Jews and Jewish refugees were there in Denmark on the ninth of April? How many Jews were uneasily approaching the future, asking questions in the same manner as the rest of the population, but with stronger fears? Julius Margolinsky [librarian of the Danish Jewish Community] has presented some statistics on the Jewish population in Denmark as it appeared during the time of the occupation. He identified a total of approximately 6,450–6,500 individuals, to which should be added individuals in mixed marriages. The Jews in Margolinsky's statistical survey fell into three groups: 1) those belonging to the very old Danish-Jewish

The king does not return the servile German soldiers' salute. He made it a habit to ignore them. Like the majority of his countrymen the king became an artful practitioner of the cold-shoulder treatment, a form of passive resistance in which Danes excelled. German parades, military concerts, and other public exhibits of German might were largely boycotted, making the Germans furious. The Germans saw themselves as "friendly neighbors" and could not comprehend the audacity of this display of the feisty and cocky, if not outrightly hostile, attitude of the Danes toward them.

community (about 1,600); 2) immigrants and their descendants, in particular those coming from Russia after 1903 (about 3,350); and 3) approximately 1,500 Jewish refugees from Germany, Austria, and Czechoslovakia. In these latter two groups, almost 2,200 individuals did not hold Danish citizenship; they were clearly the most vulnerable and most anxious about the future should the worst happen.

Within the category of noncitizens, there were two well-defined subgroups, namely 350 students of agriculture, spread across the country and living primarily in camps, and 270 Jewish children,

The king surrounded by an adoring crowd of university students on his birthday in September 1940. The trust and love felt towards him by his people, including of course the Danish Jews, reached unprecedented heights as the uncertainties of the political situation under German occupation mounted.

part of the so-called Aliyah children who had come to Denmark in the period between late summer 1939 and April 1940. Like so many refugees, both groups were only "passing through" Denmark on their way to Palestine which they hoped to enter on British certificates. They were now stranded in their temporary host country, but in contrast to many other refugees, these groups were backed by very powerful organizations—the first group by the Jewish Hechaluz organization and the latter by Danish women's organizations. The real question was how much such organizational clout was worth in the eyes of the mighty enemy in Denmark? Actually, it was possible to get a small group of agriculture students and young athletes through to Sweden during the first days of the occupation. Later, two major departures were organized for a number of children, eighty-seven in all, who traveled the long distance through Sweden, Finland, Russia, and Turkey to Palestine. For the rest, all escape routes appeared to be closed. Fortunately, as it turned out, the Danish government, in line with the conception shared by the Danish public, equated the term "Danish Jews" with "Jews in Denmark" and acted accordingly. The two terms were differentiated only for statistical purposes.

For all the Jews in Denmark—the old families who had been in Denmark for generations, the new families with roots less deep, and the refugees—the burning question now was exactly how the occupation of Denmark would be organized in view of the German government's insistence that the occupation of Denmark was merely an act of protection, even adding that "it did not—presently or in the future—aim at disturbing the teritorial integrity nor the political independence of the Kingdom of Denmark."

It was, among other things, this wording in the German ultimatum that the Danish foreign minister, Peter Munch, closely followed when, in the course of the day, he prepared his letter of protest to Germany. And it was to this formulation of German policy that the Danish government tried to hold the Germans when, in the following days, weeks, and months, it was continuously forced to negotiate with the Germans on a long series of issues that inevitably came up as a result of the occupation. The viability of the Danish government, on the one hand, and the

German interests, on the other, codetermined the future conditions that would prevail in Denmark. The division of weight was evident. The Jews, along with everyone else in Denmark, had to face facts while fearing the worst, yet hoping for a tolerable future. In this sense the Jewish fate became linked to the Danish fate. If the Danish government could sustain its avowed position that the status of Danish Jews was an internal, domestic affair, or better still, if the issue could be swept under the carpet in Danish-German negotiations, there was a faint glimmer of hope in the agonizing situation.

The Jewish leaders quickly understood this, and at a meeting on 10 April called by the Board of Representatives of the Jewish Community, it was agreed that the only option for the Jews was to have confidence in the Danish government and to take no action which could weaken the position of the government in Danish-German negotiations or bring the issue of Jewish existence into the limelight. Marcus Melchior briefly described the meeting in his memoirs, *A Rabbi Remembers* (1968), whereas the written minutes of the meeting are silent on this serious item, focusing instead on the routine matters taken up by the board.

The watchword was quietly but quickly spread and to the entire Jewish community and was everywhere accepted and heeded. Needless to say, there was a lot of anxiety among all Jews, ranging from the uneasiness experienced by the Danish population in general to a more uniquely Jewish fear. There is no evidence of panic, however. Naturally, the refugees were the ones with the greatest anxiety, but even among them, a calm gradually emerged. As calmness was in everyone's interest, the Jewish leaders did all they could to allay the anxiety among the refugees.

C. B. Henriques, himself a distinguished supreme-court lawyer, had a deep trust in the legislative and judicial structures of the Danish society, and had no doubt that the Jewish security in Denmark could be based on the Danish government's ability and determination to act as a protective buffer for the Jewish community. He recalls that:

> When people came to me and said, 'We are frightened. What should we do?' I always answered, 'Stay calm! Continue to live and behave

> as usual. Don't do anything! Anything else might be provocative and encourage counter-measures and cause harm to the Danish government, which has enough problems as it is.' This line of advice was followed. I had under my charge many immigrants who had escaped from Germany whom they [the Germans] might now go after. I managed to allay their fears though they were naturally still quite apprehensive. But everything went well. No one laid a hand on anybody.

This watchword "to stay calm" was followed by even the most radical of the Jewish groups, such as the Zionist agriculture students who were part of the Hechaluz movement and who had come to Denmark with the single goal of learning agriculture so that they could eventually realize their dream of an independent Israel in Palestine. They spent the days that followed 9 April discussing whether there were alternative courses of action, but, even here, all meetings ended with the conclusion that a wait-and-see attitude was the only way. Thus, even for them, the daily routine on the farms simply continued. Perhaps the only change was that the training in Palestinian studies intensified. As the months passed and the children of the Aliyah group matured, they became more strongly influenced by their older peers in the Hechaluz group and, through clandestine study groups, developed a firmer Zionist ideology. In this regard, these young people differed dramatically from the old Jewish families living mainly in Copenhagen who, though they were sympathetic to the dreams of these young people and supportive in a financial and practical sense, did not share their desire to leave Denmark—the country which for more than one hundred years had given them equal rights and opportunities. These old families were indeed Jewish—and made no bones about it—but through generations Denmark had become their native country, their beloved homeland. Between the two extremes in the spectrum of feelings and attitudes, many gradations could be found. In general, however, it may be said that there was an increased interest in Zionism among many of the younger Jews living in Denmark under the occupation.

As the Danish people, led by the Danish government, became the Jews' only safeguard, one had to confront the question of how strong this buffer in fact was. Here, it is important to bear in mind that it took weeks and months before a pattern emerged from the Danish-German negotiations which could help cast some light on the future of the Danish situation. It should also be born in mind that until the fall of France in June 1940 it was impossible to assess how long the occupation would last. Only after the quite unexpected collapse of the Allied armies did it become clear that the occupation would be lengthy and perhaps even develop into a permanent state of dependency on German whim. But even so, or perhaps because of it, the Jews in Denmark had to cling to the hope that the Danish government, under the German promise of political autonomy, would provide judicial-legislative protection for all its citizens. From the Jewish vantage point there was nothing to do but wait and to watch the Danish-German negotiations in extreme suspense. For the time being, the key to survival lay in the hands of the Danish government—but was this perhaps only an interlude?

The best thing to do in the meantime was to stay as invisible as possible within the bounds of one's self-respect. At board meetings of the Danish Jewish Community through May 1940, it was decided to cancel a planned fund-raising appeal for the "Jewish Committee of Refugees of May 4th, 1933," and at least for the time being to suspend the publication of the *Jewish Family Journal*. Jewish lecture programs were temporarily shelved. At the same time, however, the vice-chairman of the Jewish Community, Karl Lachmann, was authorized to spend 50,000 Danish Kroner on various other activities, such as grants and scholarships as well as aid for refugees. In fact, by 1942, the amount raised and donated had reached 350,000 kroner. The wording of the "refugee aid" item was changed to "charity" in the account books. This and other funds, including contributions from the Denmark Lodge, were distributed to various places. Of singular importance was the financial support provided for the soup kitchen for refugees which the Committee of May 4th had founded in October 1933 and which, since that time, had been run by women volunteers from the Jewish Community. The kitchen drew up to one hundred people a day, averaging about seventy. In addition, aid was provided for Hechaluz work—for refugees and any others who, due to emergency, illness, or sudden unemployment, were exposed to financial hardship or misfortune. The financial demands on the

Jewish Community's resources increased considerably, especially since aid from outside Denmark came to an abrupt end.

Support for other worthy welfare activities had to be severely cut, and soon many of the existing committees in aid of refugees dating back to the 1930s had to redirect their aims. At a board meeting on 4 September 1940, Karl Lachmann was able to report on the negotiations involving the Department of Justice and the social welfare officials in Copenhagen that resulted in the transfer of all aid for refugees from the various private committees to the Department of Social Welfare by 1 August. The soup kitchen, however, was allowed to continue operations so that refugees in need could still have their meals there, under Jewish auspices.

This was only the beginning of the final disposition. The committees in aid of refugees had come under German scrutiny. The Germans demanded that all activity cease, that the books and balance sheets be submitted to them, and that bank accounts be closed. This matter led to Danish-German negotiations in the inital months of 1941, with the result that the books, having been revised in time, were "lent" to the Germans. Further, the committees agreed to stop all activities by 1 April 1941, but requested that their assets be deposited in escrow accounts from which money could be withdrawn only by order of the Department of Justice and spent for travel expenses should that be needed for the refugees.

The German demands were directed in the first place against the Committee of May 4th, the Matteotti Committee, and the Danish Aid Committee for Exiled Intellectuals, but the activities of the Lutheran Church's Collection for Non-Aryan Exiles and the Danish Quaker Center had to stop as well. However, a single committee remained in operation, namely, the Committee for Jewish Agricultural Students, run by Binjamin Slor and Julius Margolinsky. Coolheadedly, Margolinsky, who had been in charge of the daily work of the committee through the 1930s in close collaboration with the Agricultural-Economic Travel Bureau, changed the committee's name simply to "Secretariat." He continued the work according to the guidelines which, for almost a decade, had been part of the agreement with the Travel Bureau and, through it, with the police office dealing with aliens. Having made this change, the agriculture students were now able to receive support from the committee with the innocent name, as well as from their self-established Hechaluz office which focused specifically on issues relevant to the training of the students and Hechaluz children for a life in Palestine—a vision of the future which no occupation could crush. The two offices worked closely together, overlapping and supplementing each other in various ways, the Hechaluz office being the more radical Zionist wing and the Secretariat acting as a moderate voice with a more realistic sense of the ramifications of the situation in Denmark for Jews.

Having only briefly noted that Jewish lecture programs were temporarily stopped, one must modify this statement to point out that, in fact, there was a plethora of meetings taking place in the whole country, albeit within "closed" circles. In these activities, the driving force was the Union of Danish Youth, a conglomerate of political organizations founded in the late summer, along with a number of non-political unions under Professor Hal Koch, one of the leaders. There was in this cooperative venture no natural place for the inclusion of the Jewish youth organizations, although, perhaps as a reflection of the degree of cooperation in the Danish society at large, the board of the Danish Jewish Community was informed in October 1940 that the Danish Zionist Organization, the Chaluzim in Denmark Club, the Jewish Women's Club, the Jewish Youth Club, Hakoah, and Mizrachi were proposing a cooperative effort, too, with the purpose of enhancing their effectiveness. The Jewish Community responded by provisionally granting the amount of two-hundred Danish Kroner a month for meeting activities until 1 May 1941. This grant was renewed several times allowing the Jewish organizations to participate in the ever-expanding meeting activities that sprang up in the Danish society as a democratic and consequently anti-German force. Under the leadership of Marcus Melchior, the club activities took on the form of study groups working behind closed doors, giving them a special cast of hidden freedom during the occupation.

"THERE IS NO JEWISH PROBLEM IN DENMARK"

The minor, but by no means unimportant matter of the refugee committees was typical of the particular situation which characterized Denmark during the occupation. In line with the resolution of many other matters, it points to the reality that existed, namely, that a German wish gradually sharpened into an insistent demand in Danish-German negotiations, with the gradual weakening of the Danish government's position in order to acquire at least some concessions. How firmly the government would stand on the major issues, first and foremost the status of the Jews, was of course the problematic question. For the time being, the Jewish community could only hope that the issue would not even come up, but that hope, of course, was to be found in the realm of illusion. Nevertheless, the year 1940 came to an end without anything happening. But in April 1941, Himmler, passing through Denmark on his way to Norway, had a talk with the Danish chief of police, Thune Jacobsen. During the conversation, dealing with attitudes and positions of the Danish police, Himmler added that there was also the matter of the Jewish problem in Denmark, to which Jacobsen, noting the small number of Jews in Denmark, responded that the Danish population did not consider it a problem. This reply—"There is no Jewish problem in Denmark"—became the standard Danish stance in subsequent years whenever the issue was brought up by the Germans. Whether made by politicians, civil servants, or leading public officials, the Germans soon got the message. In her book, *The Rescue of Danish Jewry* (1969), Dr. Leni Yahil mentions that there was a leading article in the official German journal *Die Judefrage* (March 1941) entitled "Denmark: A Country Without a Jewish Problem?". To quote Yahil: "The author of the article complained that the phrase 'Denmark has no Jewish problem' allowed for no discussion and suggested that a preoccupation with racial problems was considered 'un-Danish'!"[3] Besides Thune Jacobsen, there were clearly others who had dismissed the problem with that standard response.

At that point, the question or issue had not yet become a part of the Danish-German negotiations, but it is true that already then, if not even earlier, it had been considered un-Danish to discuss a matter so alien to the Danish democratic way of thinking. German representatives in Copenhagen were quite familiar with this attitude, which was to be found not only in the general population but also in the political parties and within the government. Yahil, using

German source material, presents an extremely interesting and profound historical analysis of how the German minister in Denmark, von Renthe-Fink, and later, after November 1942, the German plenipotentiary Werner Best, attempted to keep the issue out of their reports to Germany and consequently the Danish-German negotiations. The strategy of procrastination and avoidance that the German chief negotiators followed in Copenhagen had its roots in their clear understanding that the issue was not only uncomfortably sensitive, but potentially explosive. If Germany wished to keep up the illusion of "normal" Danish-German relations, it could not address the Jewish question without threatening the breakdown of the Danish-German negotiations, an outcome that would have had dire political and economic consequences for Germany. Although Yahil's analysis is both interesting and skillfully documented, it is based on hindsight. Unfortunately her data and resultant conclusions were not available at the time!

The Danes had to steer a course without this knowledge; they had to guess their way based on whatever indications they could pick up from the Germans. Every comment, even the most casual or innocent, was duly noted. The informed Jewish leaders took note of everything no less than the Danish politicians did. "It should not come as a revelation that we, like seismographers, noted every tremor in the land," stated Marcus Melchior.

And there were tremors in 1941 that were bound to be upsetting to the Jews. In numerous major and minor matters, the government felt compelled to give in to German pressure. The arrests and internment of the Communists in June 1941 must have been experienced as a violation of the very principle that motivated Danish political activity and the Danish-German negotiations, namely the protection of the legal rights of Danish citizens despite the occupation. It would seem that the government did not consider itself able to guarantee such protection in all cases; thus, in this extreme case, it allowed an infringement of the Constitution. The Communists, admittedly, were not deported but transported to the Horserød camp,[4] but nevertheless a group of Danes had been sacrificed for the sake of negotiation! By then, individual politicians, such as Christmas Møller, Hans Hedtoft, and H. C. Hansen, had been sacrificed on the same altar, and others were to follow. Where was the line to be drawn? Naturally, for the Jewish observer, every concession on the government's part bore evidence of the distressing fact that step by step the Danes were losing ground.

In the fall, another alarming event occurred in which the government felt pressured to surrender. In November 1941, after severe internal political battles, the Danish government decided to sign the Anti-Comintern Pact. (It was actually a modified version that included an addenda which specified the treaty's provisions concerning collaboration against the Communists were to be limited to the Danish police force.) Erik Scavenius, the Danish foreign minister, made a trip to Berlin to sign the treaty. During his conversation with the Nazi leaders Ribbentrop, Göring, and Hitler, the Jewish problem was touched upon with the German suggestion that the signing of a treaty was the natural solution (a point of view that was also prominent in the German newspaper editorials). Göring had introduced the issue by observing that Denmark could not avoid the Jewish problem to which Scavenius once more gave the standard Danish reply that there was no Jewish problem in Denmark.

The trip to Berlin raised the Jewish question to topical prominence, reflected in the publication of an issue of the Danish anti-Semitic smut paper *Kamptegnet*[5] which, two days after the signing of the Anti-Comintern treaty, used the opportunity to publish one of its many defamatory articles and to invite membership in the Danish Anti-Semitic League. This was followed on 20 December by an arson attempt on the synagogue in Copenhagen. The matter simply would not disappear. Nevertheless, the Danish government and politicians in the so-called Nine-Member Committee decided to table further discussions of the issue. In response to Scavenius's report on his Berlin talks, it was agreed that any mention of a legislative act in connection with the Jewish question was unacceptable. On 22 December Danish Prime Minister Stauning announced that this was also the final decision reached by his coalition cabinet of eight ministers.

News of the decision was not kept silent by the government. The Jewish leaders received official information of the decision. On 17 December, Dr. Marcus Melchior attended a special meeting of the Jewish Community board in response to the growing uneasiness with the recent events. The minutes of the board, usually rendered in a rather laconic style, provide an elaborate summary:

> The Chief Rabbi reported that, at the invitation of the Minister of Ecclesiastical Affairs, he had a meeting with him on December 8. The Minister, Fibiger, stated that these were difficult times for everyone, especially for Jews. He wanted to know what the mood was among Jews, indicating that he wished to emphasize that there was no cause for alarm. He was aware of the fact that, following the signing of the Anti-Commitern Pact, which had been forced upon the Administration, rumors of a coming legislation designed to deal with the Jewish problem had spread. The Minister stated that no one in the government would even think of going along with such legislation—because in Denmark we do not acknowledge that there is a Jewish problem. He added that the Minister for Foreign Affairs, Scavenius, fully concurred with the position that any request from the Germans in this matter would be rejected and that the Foreign Minister, if necessary, was ready to face a show-down on this issue.
>
> The Chief Rabbi had expressed his appreciation for this reassuring message. Within the Jewish community, the King and the government enjoyed full trust; in view of the good relationship that had always prevailed, it was unimaginable that special legislation could be introduced applying only to Jews. In this connection, the Chief Rabbi mentioned the shameful disgrace of the publication *Kamptegnet*. The Minister replied that the magazine ought not to be published. Though he felt that it would be inopportune for the government to ban the magazine outright, he promised that he would arrange to have it withdrawn from newstands and forbid its advertisement in public areas. The Minister once more stressed that as long as the present government was in office the Jews need have no fears.

This was the main thrust. Fibiger proceeded briefly to raise the question of whether, under the circumstances, the appointment of the Jews to leading positions in the country was desirable. Melchior replied that, though he could understand their concern, he suggested that appointments nevertheless continue to be based on qualifications in order "to insure that everyone is treated fairly."

The support of a governmental representative must have had a reassuring effect upon the Jews. Jewish morale was further strengthened shortly after when the local court handed down a severe sentence to the would-be arsonist of the synagogue. That meant that the Danish authorities, despite the fact that Denmark was occupied by the Germans, could actually sentence people on the ground of anti-Semitic activities. And, in fact, they did. When *Kamptegnet* continued its slanderous articles, the two editors, Olga v. Eggers and Aage H. Andersen, were fined and sentenced to jail on 15 May 1942, a verdict which the supreme court later upheld with an even stiffer sentence. This was undoubtedly a signal to the Germans that the government had decided to withdraw its writer's stipend (granted under the Danish Financial Act) to Olga v. Eggers. A verdict by the court was one thing, but a governmental decision was another matter—and a clear signal to the south. That the German official in Copenhagen von Renthe-Fink understood the signal and perceived *Kamptegnet* as most inconvenient for his mission in Denmark is detailed by Dr. Leni Yahil.

It should be noted that the synagogue was the target of various minor provocations. Eventually, by the fall of 1942, a twenty-four-hour guard service was established and manned by young Jewish volunteers working in close collaboration with the police. They were provided Civil Defense armbands and night sticks and had direct access to the nearest police station via an alarm system. (It says something about those days that, shortly afterwards, the insurance policy for the guards had to be canceled because the insurance company indicated the costs would be prohibitive and later the synagogue itself was closed for the winter because there was no fuel for heating.)

The Jewish people also found support from less official, but nevertheless important, quarters. Already on 13 February, 1941, Hans Hedtoft [Danish political leader and postwar prime minister] had made a major speech to the Social-Democratic Party and the labor union in which he suggested that the Jewish question was one of those issues which, if pushed by the Germans, could lead to the collapse of the Danish government. This attitude was echoed in a speech delivered by Christmas Møller [Conservative party leader] on 16 October 1941 at Hellerup Gymnasium just as Hal Koch [theologian and founder of the Union of Danish Youth] in an article published by the Union of Danish Youth magazine noted anti-Jewish ordinances as one of the major issues on which further Danish-German collaboration would come to a grinding halt. At meetings of the Union of Danish Youth in October 1941 and January 1942, the conservative leader Ole Bjørn Kraft and the moderate leader Jørgen Jørgensen made similar statements. From several other quarters, statements were made that conveyed a public consensus on this matter. To what extent it was desirable to bring up the subject at all was, of course, questionable since the very mention of it seemed to provoke an anti-Semitic response in the Nazi press.

At the Danish Jewish Community's board meeting of 17 December, Marcus Melchior reported that two independent proposals had been presented to him for consideration. One came from a clerical conference at which the suggestion was made that a representative body of the population be formed which would make a direct appeal to every democratic member of parliament requesting that they reject any potential anti-Jewish legislation. The conference participants had no doubts about the moral correctness of their initiative, but were only concerned that it be implemented at the optimal moment. In his letter to Melchior, Holger Kjær, a conference participant and a teacher from the Danish folk high school Askov, asked for Melchior's judgment on that point. The second intiative was similar to the first and was occasioned by a group of divinity students under the theologian Professor Frederick Torm. This group was also concerned with possible anti-Jewish legislation and planned a protest if such were to be introduced in parliament. Torm had informed the bishop of Zealand of the discussions that had taken place at the clerical conference and at the divinity school faculty meeting, stating that, in his judgment, it was not the appropriate time to initiate such action "since such action could readily provoke counter-action by the pro-Germans."

In addition, Torm also raised what was potentially a very tricky dilemma for the Jewish leaders: "The question of whether, in the case of an intensification of German demands, we should stand firm and run the risk of having Norwegian conditions [see Note, p. 155] introduced in Denmark—or, alternatively, would it be preferable to have a special legislation for Jews established by the Danes in which case it would not amount to very much?"

When Melchior gave a report on Torm's position and the question he had raised to the members of the Jewish Community board, their response was clear. They did not quarrel with Torm's perception of the situation; however, they pointed out that it was not possible for the Jews in Denmark to address Torm's proposed dilemma since they simply could not imagine the enactment of a special law against the Jews in Denmark. The question would have to be resolved by the competent authorities empowered to look after Denmark's welfare and dignity.

In a conversation with Torm and in a letter to Holger Kjær, the Jewish Community expressed its gratitude for the humanitarian concern they had shown, but rejected the proposed initiatives, adding that the Jewish Community would be appreciative to clergy members and others who felt the same way if they would make their views known to the members of parliament, namely, that a special law would be unacceptable and contrary to the Danish notion of human rights and individual freedom. It was a Jewish dilemma: although support was welcome, support that was too public was *not* if it brought attention to the existence of Jews. Any public comment or mention, even a minor one, would all too quickly lead the Nazi papers to meddle in a problem that was best served by silence.

The main concern, shared by everyone who gave voice to the subject, was that the negotiation policy should not lead to any legislative act that would conflict with the Danish concept of justice—or else the very foundation on which the country was established would start to crumble. The defense of the Jews was thus anchored in the Danish constitution and in Danish democracy. It may have been precisely the violation of this principle which had taken place in connection with the Communists in 1941—even though it was deemed necessary in anticipation of conflict with the Germans—that had sensitized the public to this crucial, but fragile foundation for the course set by Denmark's political stance. The foundation was fragile because no one could predict how long the Danish government could continue making its concessions. The Jewish position was to cling to the hope that things would continue on the track set by the political leadership, at least until the end of the occupation.

It is no wonder, then, that the so-called cable crisis[6] in the fall of

1942 was experienced as yet another shock. As many may know, this crisis, which was characterized by weeks of a diplomatic war of nerves, eventually led to the replacement of the government by a new and politically weaker one, headed by a new prime minister, Erik Scavenius. Scavenius was actually chosen by the Germans through their newly appointed reich commissioner in Denmark, Werner Best, whose recent arrival in Denmark made him an unknown quantity. A new German army chief, General von Hanneken, was already in place, having come with strict instructions that the *Wehrmacht* should regard itself as being in enemy territory and that any resistance had to be crushed. In the event the Danish police proved insufficient or unwilling to follow German directives, additional German SS troops would be made available.

The wording of these instructions was not known. And what the future held for the new political arrangement was similarly unknown, but it soon became apparent that at a minimum the *Wehrmacht* had set upon a sterner course, a situation that naturally aroused a new wave of anxiety among the Jews.

During those long weeks, when Danish-German relations were disrupted by the recall and expulsion of diplomatic envoys, rumor had it that there was now a serious chance that ordinances against the Jews would be introduced. Even in this situation the politicians lived up to their promise of December 1941. The outgoing Danish prime minister, Vilhelm Buhl, informed the German authorities that the establishment of anti-Jewish regulations "would be incompatible with the setting up of the new Danish government," and when Scavenius was called to Berlin for negotiations near the end of the crisis, he too affirmed, at a meeting of Danish cabinet ministers prior to his departure, that the raising of the Jewish question would preclude the formation of any government. As it turned out, the Jewish question was not raised in Berlin, and when the negotiations a few days later were transferred to Copenhagen, with Werner Best and Scavenius as negotiators, the silence on the Jewish question was maintained. These negotiations led to a Scavenius government as the only viable possibility, but before he was given final approval to form a new cabinet, he was queried under oath, by the retiring ministers, on four key issues, one of which concerned the prospective government's stance on anti-

Jewish legislation. The atmosphere at the meeting was tense, with Scavenius objecting strenuously to playing the role of a suspect in hearings that resembled a coronation charter. He declared, however, that he was opposed to any special legislation pertaining to Jews, although he was inclined to propose that promotions of Jews [serving in the public or professional sector] be suspended and that the performance or appearance of Jews on the radio or other public forums be curtailed. The context for his position—actually not an unreasonable one given the situation—was that during 1942 a number of German attempts had been made to remove Jews from key positions. Scavenius, along with others, had repulsed these demands by consistently pointing to the fact that such anti-Jewish ordinances were not acceptable to the Danish people who would inevitably perceive these as a negation of Denmark's basic principles. In view of the German demands and bearing in mind the Jewish leaders' eagerness not to increase the already existing tension, Scavenius's attempt to exercise caution by having Jews keep a low profile was not unreasonable. These were, nevertheless, matters of principle. Every single instance of encroachment on Denmark's basic principle had been warded off by the Danes. However, when viewed within the larger context of Denmark's conflicts with Germany during the occupation, the issue of encroachment or nonencroachment alone did not really have the weight to increase significantly the explosiveness of the conflict.

THE FATAL YEAR OF 1943

Although the fall of 1942 had been full of political tension and disturbing incidents, the spring of 1943 was unexpectedly peaceful. Much to everyone's surprise Werner Best was prepared to take a moderate course in Denmark. Recognizing the general attitude in the country, he continued to take the approach of his predecessors on the Jewish question; he did his best to ensure that it did not surface. The Jews even saw *Kamptegnet* cease its publication in May 1942; Best allowed it to go bankrupt after a financial tug-of-war. In March, Danish Jews voted in the general election, an election which had proceeded in a manner that perhaps was not quite constitutional, but nevertheless indicative of a lessening

By early August 1943, general unrest across the land caused bloody clashes between the people and the Danish police. Here a police van is being overturned by citizens in Odense. The Danish government, which from the beginning of the occupation was resigned to a policy of cooperation and negotiation (within carefully delineated boundaries), issued urgent appeals for an end to the escalation of sabotage, labor unrest, strikes, and anti-German demonstrations.

of tension and yielding results that showed a clear democratic leaning among the voters. The Danish Nazi party, DNSAP, was the big loser in the election, making it abundantly clear to everyone, including Best, that the party had ceased to be a political factor.

But other conditions were to characterize the spring. By the beginning of 1943, events at Stalingrad, in Africa, as well as in the Pacific Ocean clearly found the glory of the axis powers waning. Even without the benefit of hindsight, people seemed to feel that the final defeat of the axis powers was close at hand.

There was yet another condition to reckon with. A Danish resistance movement was in the process of becoming a significant force. The illegal press had long been a reality, and still other underground resistance activities were reaching maximum development. There were constant improvements in sabotage activities, using British

Street fights and demonstration continued unabated during August 1943. Here, people scurry for safety lest they be caught in the cross fire between protesters and the police. The Germans menacingly brought out their heavy artillery and tanks in a show of might as they pressed their demands on the governement. But to no avail. The concessions already exacted by the Germans on military, economic, political, judicial, and even cultural fronts were finally too much for the people: the decisive collapse of the government occurred on 29 August 1943. The so-called soft, moderate, and "correct" approach to Denmark (Hitler's "model protectorate") ended.

supplies of explosives. Following in the wake of this, there was an increase in unrest and turmoil, which, in the summer of 1943 culminated in a number of countrywide strikes that led to confrontations between Danish demonstrators and German soldiers.

The Jewish attitudes toward these developments surely had to be ambivalent. On the one hand, it must have been satisfying to know that the Germans were having more and more difficulties, but on the other hand, these developments necessarily weakened the government's position, the very position on which the Jews had placed their trust. Were the government to collapse, the Jews would inevitably be the most vulnerable group in the population. The recent developments were thus both welcome and upsetting. For obvious reasons, to participate in the resistance movement was out of the question for Jews, especially for the many Jewish refugees, but, in general, Jewish participation was also contrary to the Jewish leadership's strategy which called for trustful loyalty to the government. Even minor indications of Jewish resistance activity could have, and most likely would have, carried severe consequences for the whole Jewish community.

The dilemma was undoubtedly intensified by the growing awareness of the inhuman treatment of European Jewry by the Germans. Though the full extent of the "final solution," already in full gear, was unknown, it was common knowledge that a horrible tragedy was unfolding elsewhere in Europe. Among other things, the fate of several hundred Norwegian Jews was now known. They had been deported in December 1942 and March 1943 to German camps.

Living under these conditions and circumstances, was there really anything to do but toe the line, finding satisfaction in every German setback and fearing the consequences? The Jewish leaders in Copenhagen did not change their set course nor see any realistic alternative other than to hope for the best passively, while fearing the worst. There was, however, one group of Jews whose members neither could nor would sit still and accept the role of the helpless victims. With resistance work closed off to them, except for the distribution of illegal newspapers (the anxiety of the larger Jewish community being one of several reasons for not getting more involved), this group's energy and determination had to find another, and for them even more relevant, outlet. Within the group of agricultural students, a subgroup of about fifty eager beavers were hell-bent on exploring a way out of the German-dominated continent of Europe to Palestine. Their goal in coming to Denmark had been to prepare for a future in Palestine and the creation of an independent state of Israel. With their strong Zionist ideals, they had found themselves stranded in a country that was never to become their own; some among them were outspoken in their rejection of the shelter provided by an administration that was not theirs. Infused with Zionism, the group differed markedly from the established Jewish community in Denmark.

The result was a number of death-defying preliminary attempts to cross the continent to Turkey and ultimately to Palestine. An early method involved crawling under a train into the substructure, staying wedged in the iron construction between the wheels—even armed with adequate food and drink for a long journey, this was a feat requiring considerable robustness, not to mention courage. This mode of travel allowed the first who tried it to reach far south into Europe, but ended in tragedy. When Bertil Grass, the leader of the group, reached Sofia in Bulgaria and was on his way back to report his success, he was caught in Hamburg. It was a journey with no return; his life ended in Auschwitz. A new method was explored—hiding in large crates that presumably contained machines for export to Turkey. This attempt too went awry; five who tried to escape this way were arrested in Germany and sent to Auschwitz. There was only a single survivor who was able to give an account of the horrors they experienced. A detailed description of the various ways this group tried to blaze "*Der Neue Weg*" ["the New Path"] may be found in Uri Yarii's book *Konfrontationer* [*Confrontations*].

The idea of getting out of what the group must have perceived as the Danish "trap" was not relinquished. At a meeting in Sorø, the group was dissolved in favor of individual initiatives—and the idea of escaping to Sweden made its appearance. Three of the Hechaluz members were trained as fishermen on Bornholm [a Danish island]. On 31 March 1943, they boarded a small cutter in Tejn and, in the storm and dark of night, piloted out of the harbor, raised the sails, and after a short period of wind navigation switched to power. Six hours later they docked at the port of Simrishamn in Sweden.

The escape proved that flight to Sweden was feasible. The Jewish fishermen quickly set out to obtain a cutter in Sweden in order to return to the Danish coast and rescue other Hechaluz friends. In light of our present knowledge of the numerous crossings that were to occur later on, it might seem superfluous to have to demonstrate the viability of such an escape route, but the fact is that,

The Danish coastline, heavily guarded by Germans who immediately took over many Danish military forts. Though they allowed the Danish military, border, and palace guards to continue in place, subject to German will, they carefully monitored the Danish coast guards' surveillance of sea traffic, in addition to instituting their own heavy mining and patrol efforts. Escape to nearby Sweden was thus extremely dangerous, if not virtually unthinkable, during the first three years of the occupation. And Sweden did not yet have its welcome mat out; its "neutrality" favored Germany.

up until late summer 1943, illegal traffic to Sweden had been considered near impossible. A few individuals crossed the ice to Sweden in the winter and a few others had tried kayaks, rubber boats, and similar means of transportation; in fact, in the summer of 1943, inflatable rubber boats were being dropped by English planes for that purpose. Rubber boats were expensive, as were kayaks, and only a few succeeded in crossing the Øresund. The coastline was patrolled by the Danish coast guard until 29 August 1943 and was considered impenetrable, except by sheer luck and at the risk of one's life.

The fishing boat from Tejn was the first sign of things to come, but it also occasioned a serious warning to the Jewish Community. The Germans, who promptly had received news of the escape to Sweden, warned the Jewish leadership through two Danish officials. The Jewish leaders, in turn, passed the word down to the Hechaluz group, to cease further escape activity. Binjamin Slor negotiated with the leaders of the Hechaluz office, and Julius Margolinsky issued an extensive written warning to the group across the country. The daring escape of a small group of agriculture students had placed the entire Jewish Community in a situation of high risk. Under the circumstances, they would simply have to do what was best for the majority of the Jewish community. Margolinsky's letter was sharply critical and condemning of those involved in *Der Neue Weg*. He characterized their activities as immature, irresponsible, and adventurous. When one considers Margolinsky's close relationship to the group and his deep appreciation of Zionism, the tone of the letter is strikingly caustic. Also striking is a passage in the letter stating that "there has been no reasonable cause for setting any conditions on the agricultural training in Denmark"—a view which he reaffirmed in letters sent to Danes who had close contact with the students. In these letters he asked that they make the students understand that attempts at illegal escape were intolerable, adding "there has been absolutely no reason for such escapes, isn't that so?"

This was the attitude prevailing in Copenhagen and was consistent with the position of the Jewish leadership. It was testimony to the degree of confidence these leaders still, in April 1943, had in the government's pledge of protection. This confidence was the positive side of the Jewish attitude, but there was a negative side as well. Karl Lachmann [vice-chairman of the Jewish Community board], on the topic of a possible escape, put it as follows:

> It was generally agreed that it should be avoided. It was not feasible to hide 6000 to 7000 people. Every move would require help from non-Jewish citizens which one could neither ask for nor expect to receive. No one could possibly have imagined that Sweden would take in such a large group of people. All that would be accomplished by trying to escape would be chaos and panic, as well as an excuse for German reprisals. The question of rescuing Jewish children was given the same answer.

THE BEGINNING OF THE ACTION AGAINST THE JEWS

Four months later, the positive assumption inherent in the Jewish position and deliberations was to explode, while the more negative anticipations regarding mass escape were to be proven false in light of Danish reality. On 28 August 1943, in the wake of widespread riots and intensification of resistance activities, the government was faced with an unacceptable German ultimatum. In consultation with the other political parties, the government determined that it had no choice; it had to resign. The path was now clear for a German takeover of all power. A state of emergency was declared, serious attacks on the Danish garrison took place, the Danish military personnel were disarmed, and several leading public figures were seized as hostages, among them three Jewish leaders—Chief Rabbi Dr. M. Friediger, C. B. Henriques, and Axel Margolinsky.

For the Jews in Denmark this was a catastrophe. Now, there was undeniably a sound reason for escape. The question was whether it was possible, and, if so, how and when. Even now the Jewish leaders hesitated despite the fact that the weeks following 29 August brought some ominous warnings.

On 31 August, a break-in took place in the law office of attorney Arthur Henriques where three armed men forcibly took possession of the Jewish Community files. The break-in was immediately reported to the police and brought to the attention of Nils Svenningsen [who in the absence of a cabinet ministry was running the Foreign Office]. Protests were issued to Werner Best demanding an explanation not only of the incident in Henriques's office but also of the situation in general: Were there to be special ordinances applying to Jews? Best was evasive. He didn't know anything about the matter nor was there talk of raising the Jewish question in Denmark! Best's denial contained the following wording: "The Jewish question has, up to now, not been touched on at all." He promised a German investigation of the incident which was never undertaken. Perhaps the categorical expression "not at all" overshadowed the ominous qualifier "up to now."

The break-in naturally caused alarm among Jews, but still the leaders hesitated. The records of the Jewish Community contain this entry from 8 September: "According to the available information, it must be assumed that the break-in was perpetrated by

On 29 August 1943 the Germans declared a state of emergency, disarmed the Danish military force, arrested officers, and took a number of prominent Danes hostages—professors, editors, members of parliament, businessmen, writers—leaders of the Jewish community among them. Here, they are unceremoniously hauled aboard "prairie wagons" during the early morning hours and taken to Horserød prison camp, north of Copenhagen.

individuals acting on their own, taking advantage of the state of emergency." The Jewish Community had been exposed to harrassment before. It still clung to the slim thread of hope that a new government might be formed, much as the power of wishful thinking must have led it to overlook the "up to now" in the German words of denial.

But on 17 September, yet another more serious event occurred which could not be passed off as the work of individuals acting on their own. A German police car with German soldiers raided the Jewish Community offices in Ny Kongensgade, picked up the archivist-librarian, Josef Fischer, conducted a thorough search of the offices, and ultimately impounded books and archival rec-

The royal guards are replaced by German sentries; the king is under house arrest. As tension and uncertainty gripped the country, Denmark's Jews became acutely concerned about their fate, their protective government and king no longer in place. Some went into hiding, others simply worried or hoped for the best. The idea that persecution of Jews could happen in Denmark was still too far-fetched for most.

ords. Once again a report was made to the Danish Foreign Office, and once more the German authorities made light of the matter, reiterating that there was no question of an action against the Jews. Parenthetically, the search had yielded rather meager results. At a board meeting on 8 September, a decision had been made to store the Jewish Community records in the regional archival office and to deposit current files with the National Archival Office for photocopying.

Still the leaders were in the grip of indecision born of their belief that a mass escape to Sweden was impossible and their hope that a new Danish government, or at least a caretaker Danish administration, would continue to serve as a protective shield for the Jews in the country.

But the hour had already struck. On 8 September, Best had sent a cable to Berlin in which he recommended that the time was ripe for dealing with the Jewish question in Denmark. This cable had been the trigger for the catastrophic events to come. Ten days later Hitler issued the order for the action. There remained only the determination of the nature and the date of the action. The date was set by the German command in Denmark for the night of 1 and 2 October.

In this article on the Jews during the occupation, brief as it is, it is impossible to go into the incredibly complicated details of the internal communications which characterized the impenetrable German hierarchy. In her book, *Rescue of Danish Jewry,* Leni Yahil has provided such an account based on sources that the war's end made available. It was, she concludes, Best's cable that triggered the catastrophe for which, later, almost everyone within the German hierarchy was to deny responsibility. These historically interesting details are not, however, that relevant here. What matters in this context is the question: What did the Jews know about all this at the time? *They knew absolutely nothing!*

They first learned what was afoot when Duckwitz, the sole decent person among the German leaders, tried, at great personal risk, to have the cable stopped in Berlin, to warn the Swedish government, and, as a last decisive measure, to pass along a warning to his Social-Democratic friends, Hans Hedtoft and H. C. Hansen, through whom the message reached C. B. Henriques and Marcus Melchior on 28 September. This warning, which spread like lightning, spelled the rescue for thousands.

If the Jews had no knowledge of the events leading up to Duckwitz's warning, neither did the Danish caretaker administration. By the last week of September, it became clear that no new Danish government would be formed, but that instead the country would be administered under Danish law by department heads of the various ministries. It was this sort of Danish caretaker government that the Jewish leaders had anticipated as their last chance. And when Svenningsen, department head in the foreign affairs ministry, also received Duckwitz's warning on 29 September, there was a last-ditch, and hopeless, effort at negotiation between

Dr. Werner Best, the German plentipotentiary and SS Obergruppenführer, is seen here standing between two Danish Nazis. His motives for sending the fateful telegram to Ribbentrop on 8 September 1943 that instigated the action against the Danish Jews are still controversial. The Danish Nazis were politically and numerically quite insignificant. Nevertheless they constituted a source of terror, countersabotage, and anti-Semitic provocation. Some of these hated traitors joined a voluntary German army corps, others were members of the "Hipo" corps—an auxiliary police force which carried out the Germans' dirty work locally.

Svenningsen and the Jewish leaders Henriques, Lachmann, and Dr. Adolph Meyer.

These negotiations must have been chaotic. The Danish administration had only one weapon left—to negotiate with Best, who throughout September had denied that the Jewish question was on the German agenda. But if the warning was true, then what value did that weapon hold? The more realistic solution—an illegal mass escape across the Øresund—could not be raised within the legal framework of the adminstration offices. The viability of such a solution was in any case more dependent on the Danish public than on the officials. A desperate, but fleeting suggestion of the internment of the Danish Jews came up at a subsequent meeting of the heads of the Danish administration, but it was shelved as constituting an absolutely last-minute possibility. For the time being, the only advice one could give Jews was to stay away from their homes and bide their time, a piece of advice many Jews were already heeding without having to be pressed. That the idea of placing Jews in an internment camp could arise at all was, of course, due to the prior experience with the Communists who were interned in Horserød, an internment that had succeeded in preventing their being deported to German camps. On 29 September it was not yet known that they were soon to undergo mass deportation. The suggestion of Jewish internment must be viewed in this light; four days after the suggestion was introduced everyone was far wiser.

Svenningsen must have had a faint hope that the warning was baseless. Late in the afternoon he set out with Eivind Larsen [head of the justice department] to Dagmarhus [German headquarters in Copenhagen] to seek clarification from Best. At this meeting Best lied shamelessly. He evasively skirted the dreaded topic and, when asked point blank about it, maintained that the "present German authorities did not have any plans," adding, however, that "it is, of course, always difficult to issue guarantees that nothing will happen." After the war, when Best pleaded his innocence, he forgot—as did the court—this downright deception, perpetrated in a situation where it would not have been out of the question, or overly dangerous, to let the truth seep through.

The illegal solution was now the only one left. It, too, has been the subject of many books and cannot be detailed in a brief account. For an extensive treatment of the escape consult the work of Leni Yahil, the book *October 43* by Aage Bertelsen, and my own book on the agricultural students, *Passage to Palestine*.

A basic precondition for the escape will be mentioned here. There was only one truly significant background factor that made mass escape possible within reasonable limits of risk: the German action itself! The escape which was to have preceded a German action actually had to await it. A paradox of those tragic days! However, a number of other preconditions had been set in motion during the days and weeks preceding the event itself. First, the mood of the country was already at a boiling point and had been ever since the violent strikes and turmoil in the summer of 1943. The resignation of the government bore evidence of the intensity of the national mood. The vast majority of the population felt provoked and frustrated to the point where its suppressed desire for retaliation was ready to be unleashed—if the opportunity arose. Other factors were at work as well. The resignation of the government had resulted in a decisive change in the security along the Danish coasts. On the morning of 29 August, Eivind Larsen had conveyed to Paul Kanstein [chief of German security] that the Danish police would no longer consider acts by Danish citizens against the occupation forces as part of their duties. This meant that the Danish coastal police from now on would turn a blind eye to the traffic across the sound; the best of the coastal police reversed their objective—from apprehending refugees to spotting German patrols. And, finally, on 29 September, the last precondition was established. The Swedish ambassador, von Dardell, announced to Henriques that Sweden would be open to all Jewish refugees, a message which also reached Jews and the population via other channels as well. The time was ripe for the Swedes to reevaluate their political position.

The criminal action against the Jews could not have been executed at a more opportune time. The rescue effort and mass exodus, though for the most part remarkably successful, could not have succeeded in 1942.

I shall only mention the rescue in terms of the statistics collected by Julius Margolinsky after the Jews reached Swedish soil. All told, approximately 7,900 people managed to escape, of whom 686 took flight because they were married to Jews. This rescue is viewed, for many reasons, as an extraordinary episode in Danish history. From a historian's point of view, the hastily improvised escape is remarkable in that not a trace of archival material was left behind in Denmark—no passenger lists, no reports, no letters, accounts, or diaries. The hectic activity of those October weeks must be pieced together from testimony obtained from the rescued and the rescuers. However, such accounts are substantial, numbering some 150 of which about 130 are by the rescued persons themselves. They paint a singular portrait of Denmark. It is easy to understand that Jewish families firmly entrenched in Copenhagen had an easier time making arrangements for their flight to Sweden than those living in the country, though nothing was really easy in those days. By far the greater number had to seek their escape opportunity through many contacts within the Danish society, often quite casual or accidental ones. Many Jews describe as many as ten to twenty contacts preparatory to the final steps on the beach and ultimate safety. Though it is difficult to estimate, it is quite clear that tens of thousands were behind the rescue effort, often people who had not been involved previously in illegal activities. The last major rescue effort in Copenhagen, hastily improvised, was carried out by people who were in, or were about to join, the underground movement, but thousands of others came unexpectedly face-to-face with illegal action—and they passed the test with flying colors. What emerges is the distinct impression that it was the entire population that stood behind the rescue effort and behind the organizations that fueled the efforts in Copenhagen and along the coastline, from Gilleleje to Stubbekøbing. One should not fail to mention the hospitals in Copenhagen which served as centers of organized rescue work.

It should be evident that to approximate the number of helpers in the rescue effort is impossible. From the many accounts of the agricultural students and the Aliyah children—some 550 in all—it would seem that in their rescue alone thousands of Danes were involved in providing warnings, food and shelter, transportation, courier service, and money. The accounts of these young people make reference to those who helped as being men and women, rich and poor, old and young, urban and rural. Frequently, but not always, an organized resistance group was located in the harbor area or on the beaches. Most frequently, the helpers were described simply as "the farmer" "the young man," "the Danes," "people I did not know," "a man named Hansen," "a friendly family," "a lady," "some coast guards"—and the all-important person on the road to ultimate rescue, "the captain." Countless, but nameless individuals from all corners of the islands and from all social strata turn up in the testimonial accounts. Most of the informants were able to sense, behind the apparent chaos, the organized resistance movement, which was in reality responsible, if not in the beginning, certainly by the end of the rescue effort. Sadly, not everyone was to experience the lights of Sweden. There were Jews who did not receive the warning, who did not respond to it, or who were unable to respond quickly enough because of age or other reasons. On the day of the action, the Germans managed to arrest 284 Jews and in the following weeks of the manhunt an additional 190 were arrested while trying to arrange an escape. The German patrols were not idle; they did not work in vain. Three transports took the prisoners to the Theresienstadt concentration camp in Czechoslovakia. A few died during the transport, and a small number were returned home upon the intervention by the Danish administration. The total number of deported Jews, thus, amounted to 464, of which 101 were refugees who did not hold Danish citizenship. Fifty-one of the deported persons died in the camp while the rest returned home in 1945.

The horrors of Theresienstadt will not be described here. They have been recounted by Dr. M. Friediger in his book *Theresienstadt,* by Mélanie Oppenhejm in her work *Menneskefælden* [*The Human Trap*], and by Ralph Oppenhejm in his book *Det Skulle Saa Være* [*It Came to Pass*].

The deported were not forgotten in Denmark. Immediately after the action took place, protests were issued by a large number of influential groups in Denmark. The department heads of the administration, in their protest, demanded a guarantee that no new roundups of half-Jews or others would take place. At the same time Dagmarhus was pressed for permission to have Red Cross packages forwarded to the camp, which, despite German refusal, was arranged—first clothing, then later food. In my book *Til Landets Bedste,* [For the Country's Best], I have dealt with the considerable work that was carried out on behalf of the deported. Suffice it to say here that between October 1943 and April 1945 the

Danish administration did not let a week pass by without pressure on the German authorities—in Copenhagen as well as Berlin—to obtain the release of all those deported, to secure the right to inspect the camp at Theresienstadt, and to rectify mistakes, but first and foremost, to insure the survival of the Jews in the German camp through a regular shipment of packages. The shipments had first been a function of a private charity organization, but it was rapidly taken over by the Danish Department of Social Welfare under its chief, H. H. Koch, and his aides, Mogens Kirstein and Finn Nielsen, with the support of numerous other people in various institutions, organizations, and private companies.

How effective this continuous pressure on the Germans was is difficult to say, but at least they were never left in peace. They were constantly asked to account for the Jews deported and queried about their exact address, their fate, and welfare. Realistically, the Germans could, of course, do as they wished, but they could not do so without feeling monitored on a day by day basis. It is then a matter of judgment exactly how big a role Danish pressure played in shaping German conduct. There is good evidence to suggest that this long-distance monitoring was effective. For not one of the Jews deported from Denmark—not even the stateless refugees—was moved to the death camps, and all received packages. At no time did the administration in Copenhagen give up its hope of bringing those deported back. In fact, as early as the fall of 1943, a Danish rescue corps was established which had at its disposal transportation, drivers, physicians, nurses, food, and medical aid. When Folke Bernadotte's humanitarian exchange mission got off the ground in the spring of 1945, he was able within days to draw on contacts, equipment and supplies, and personnel in Denmark—the country that assumed the fate of the Jews as a Danish responsibility. The "white buses"[7] came to symbolize the relief activity provided those in Theresienstadt, but the many wheels and helping hands were the result of the indefatigable preparation of the Danish adminstration.

Though the Danish government, in the end, was not able to protect the civil rights of the Jews, as long as the government was in place, it was as reliable as its word. Others have since taken over the reins of power, fully cognizant that the fate of the Danish Jews was and is a Danish responsibility.

NOTES

1. In preparing this chapter Professor Hæstrup has made use of his extensive collection of archival material—letters, interviews, unpublished government reports, the Ole Barfoed collection, relevant testimony from the Nuremburg trial and from the Yad Vashem files. Where no specific source is provided for a given quotation, the reader is directed to this archival data base, which is on deposit with the Danish State Archives.

2. Melchior, pp. 163–64.

3. Yahil, pp. 42–43.

4. Horserød camp was a detention center maintained by the Danish prison system where conditions were quite reasonable.

5. *Kamptegnet* was a weekly newspaper financially subsidized by the Germans, with a circulation of twelve-thousand at its maximum.

6. The pretext for the change in Danish-German relations was a terse cable sent by King Christian X ("My utmost thanks. Christian Rex") in response to Hitler's birthday cable to the king on his seventy-second birthday, 26 September 1942. The telegram, which was, in fact, standard in its formal and aloof tone, presumably so enraged the Führer that neither apology nor appeasement could undo the insult. Instead, Hitler instituted a new and much tougher stance toward Denmark's governance.

7. This is a reference to the convoy of white buses in which 423 Danish Jews were transported from Theresienstadt to Sweden on 15 April 1945, following Sweden's Count Folke Bernadotte's exchange arrangement with Himmler.

REFERENCES

Bertelsen, Aage. *October, 1943*. New York: Putnam, 1954.

Friediger, Max. *Theresienstadt*. Copenhagen: J. Fr. Clausens Forlag, 1946. (Not available in English.)

Hæstrup, Jørgen. *Passage to Palestine: Young Jews in Denmark, 1932–1945*. Odense: Odense University Press, 1983.

———. *Til Landets Bedste*. Copenhagen: Gyldendal, vol. 1, 1966; vol. 2, 1971. (Not available in English.)

Melchior, Marcus. *A Rabbi Remembers*. New York: Lyle Stuart, 1968.

Oppenhejm, Mélanie. *Menneskefælden*. Copenhagen: Hans Reitzel, 1980. (Not available in English.)

Oppenhejm, Ralph. *Det Skulle Saa Være*. Copenhagen: H. Hirschsprung, 1945. (Not available in English.)

Yahil, Leni. *The Rescue of the Danish Jewry: Test of a Democracy*. Philadelphia: Jewish Publication Society of America, 1969.

Yarri, Uri. *Konfrontationer*. Copenhagen: Munksgard, 1980. (Not available in English.)

Bent Melchior, the current chief rabbi of Denmark. The son of Dr. Marcus Melchior, he has an intimate knowledge of the Jewish community and its history. He serves as chairman of Tribute To The Danes' fellowship committee.

3.

THE DANISH JEWS IN THE TWENTIETH CENTURY

Rabbi Bent Melchior

The writing of contemporary history must inevitably be undertaken with some reservation, insofar as the author often will have been so close to the events that his subjectivity will play too large a role in his assessments. Of course, no history can—or ought to—be written without subjectivity, but the issue is, rather, the breadth of perspective and richer source material that distance tends to bring in its wake.

Not being a professional historian, and in view of my own intense involvement—as well as the involvement of several generations of my ancestors—with the welfare of the Danish Jewish Community, it would be even more unthinkable that I could tackle the topic at hand without giving it my subjective cast, despite my best efforts at objectivity. This cautionary caveat with which I have prefaced this chapter is to be kept in mind also by readers belonging to future generations.

The Danish Jewish Community is as much part of Danish society as it is of the broader Jewish fellowship. Thus, it is to a large

Reprinted from Harald Jørgensen, ed., *Indenfor Murene: Jødisk liv i Danmark 1684–1984*. (Copenhagen: Selskabet for dansk jødisk Historie, C. A. Reitzels Forlag, 1984). Reprinted by permission of the author. Translated by Leo Goldberger. Editor's interpolations appear in brackets.

extent affected by events taking place in Denmark, as well as by those in the Jewish world at large. This was evident during the German occupation (1940–1945), as well as during the influx of Jews from Eastern Europe at the turn of the century. The period 1940–1945 will here be touched upon only lightly, since Dr. Hæstrup has contributed a chapter on that subject.

In the larger context, a variety of factors are intertwined and cannot be readily separated, but it should be acknowledged at the outset that without significant growth from the outside world, the Danish Jewish Community at its three hundredth jubilee [which it celebrated in 1984] would have been a curiosity rather than a vigorous community. By and large the growth came in three waves: The first was the result of the pogroms in Russia and ended, by and large, with World War I; the second was caused by the Nazi takeover in Germany and ended with World War II; the third wave was occasioned by a new and sudden outburst of anti-Semitism in Poland in the wake of Israel's "Six Days War" in 1967, and it largely ebbed in the mid-seventies.

The first wave of immigrants was the most significant in terms of sheer number. These immigrants were people with a strong Jewish background, which had provided them a considerable degree of Jewish education, religious as well as cultural, and which in turn was to have an impact on the third generation, their grandchildren. In many ways the Jews of the third generation experienced a renaissance of Jewish identity, unencumbered by the complexes that had led the second generation to distance itself from anything regarded as alien to a Danish way of life—such as "Jewishness". The ability to organize and establish a framework for their cultural activities, so characteristic of the Eastern European immigrants, was also a factor in the lasting impact they had on the Danish Jewish Community's development.

The immigration of German Jews in the 1930s was of a different nature and had a different background. Actually the younger German Jews were only in transit. The older ones were better educated, in a secular sense, than the Eastern European Jews had been, but they were on the whole also more assimilated. Furthermore, they had come to a Denmark in which they were faced with political difficulties, which spelled economic consequences of such proportions that they must have felt devastated and isolated. For them it must have been a particularly stressful and humiliating experience to weather poverty, because they had been accustomed to a high standard of living.

The last wave of immigrants is still so new in Denmark that one cannot really make an assessment of its significance for the Jewish Community. There is no doubt, however, that these are immigrants who upon their arrival were burdened with severe inner turmoil. The older ones were saddled with a sense of disillusionment, having been disappointed by the new Poland, while the younger ones had come without any Jewish core identity (in a few instances the fact of being Jewish had been hidden from the children by the parents). In comparison to earlier groups of immigrants, the rate of mixed marriages was also considerably higher. Quite a few of the new arrivals here, nevertheless, held their own in the activity of the Jewish Community as well as in Danish society generally.

In this connection it ought to be noted that throughout most of this century it was the so-called old Danish Jews who carried on the work of the Jewish Community and substantially bore the financial brunt. These were respected and able individuals, imbued with a dignified sense of piety and a worldliness, which in large measure had contributed to the fact that many Danes failed to perceive a distinction between Jew and Gentile among themselves. What this has meant in times of crisis cannot be sufficiently appreciated or overestimated.

In relationship to the waves of immigrants there was, however, the pervasive fear that they—the foreigners—would significantly disrupt the *status quo* of the old Danish Jews. The fear was in all likelihood groundless, or at least blown out of proportion, as is evidenced in the following excerpt from an article in the leading Danish paper *Berlingske Tidende,* 7 September 1913:

> The keen observer of children at play in our parks could not help, on Whitsunday, but be struck by the many children of Polish and Russian Jewish families who had found a joyful playground in the "King's Garden" [a public park in central Copenhagen].
>
> From the Polish and Russian neighborhood close by the Garden, they seemed to have pre-arranged to meet each other here—every-

> one—the adults ranging from the old grandmothers with shawls draped around their heads to the young mothers suckling their babies—appeared to have fun and to enjoy themselves. There was a sense of belonging about the group—a small community—joined in solidarity, and they were happy sharing this feeling, happy watching their children romp and play. They cheered the children on in their play by lively shouts and clapping of hands. The children were dancing, often in a strikingly graceful manner.
>
> They were all clean and neatly dressed. The hair of the young matrons was done up beautifully. The childrens' profusive hair was tied with colorful ribbons that often came undone while playing, revealing how long their hair was.
>
> No rudeness, no attempt to tease one another, no fights, no damage wrought to benches or plants. They arrived quietly and happily, quietly and happily they parted, late, at closing time.

Parenthetically, the article, written by Mrs. Emma Kraft, continues with a description of the "Jewish Children's Summer Camp built on land donated by a [Jewish] merchant named Metz," and "located in the Hellebæk area" [north of Copenhagen, near Elsinore] where Jewish children over many years were to spend their summers and fortify their health—measured in those days by the amount of weight gained by the children.

There was thus no real ground for the fear that the public at large might respond anti-Semitically to the influx of new groups of Jewish immigrants. But the fear was nevertheless a reality and played a significant role in the life of the Jewish Community until the outbreak of World War II. The appeal that Zionism held for an expanded group of Jews living in Denmark was an additional threat to the more assimilated Jews, who viewed Zionism as yet another alienating factor in their existing relationship to Gentiles. This concern is exemplified in the following excerpt from a letter to the *Jødisk Familieblad* [a monthly publication of the Danish Jewish Community] of January 1934, written by Frans Henriques [an "old" Danish Jew] in reply to an article by Nathan Skorochod [an Eastern European immigrant]:

> Assimilation was and is a fact. . . .
>
> That was the way of the Community which so hospitably received the large influx of immigrants. . . .

> And it is now in your hands, the hands of the coming generation of young foreign-born Jews, to make sure that you, and in particular your future children, inoffensively and smoothly fit into the population of our hospitable country. It is up to you to decide whether you want to live and work peacefully or whether you, by rude, arrogant, or provocative behavior or by your sheer number, will give rise to anti-Semitism and thus eventually endanger your own existence and cause deleterious damage to the status of Danish Jews. . . .
>
> It is of course understandable that the events in Germany have been upsetting to Jews. Many have reacted by becoming attracted to the ideal of the Nationalistic Jew that Skorochod has professed to identify himself with. And it is not that I underrate the justification for the attraction: If a family is driven from country to country and one has no roots anywhere, there is a tendency to cling to one's religion and family tradition. If one thus entertains the Palestinian dream one becomes a Nationalistic Jew. . . .
>
> It is quite logical and understandable. . . . However, one must then be prepared to take the consequences and take cognizance of the fact that a Nationalistic Jew of non-Danish origin is after all only a guest in Denmark and as such is expected to behave as a well-behaved guest should in an accommodating and hospitable home—that is: not to make demands! . . .
>
> So let it be said loud and clear: A Nationalistic Jew of foreign origin has no claim to Danish citizenship nor to its advantages under Danish law.

But viewpoints also prevailed in the 1930s that at least in some areas served to balance the picture. It was, not surprisingly, most evident among the young, who in 1934 succeeded in uniting three independent clubs into the Jewish Youth Organization, thereby breaking down some old barriers. The result was an energetic organization which in subsequent decades came to serve not only the young, but also other members of the community, as a meeting place and framework for many cultural and social events. Soon the leaders of the new organization also set the lead for The Scandinavian Jewish Youth Organization and for such highlights as annual summer camps and congresses under Scandinavian auspices. After World War II, the Jewish Youth Organization initiated a highly visible activity—the selection of outstanding individuals for the Ben Adam award. The award ceremony customarily took place at special festivities and banquets. Needless to say, the fact that the Danish Nobel laureate Niels Bohr became a Ben Adam title recipient (in 1951) added quite a luster to the award.

In addition, the 1930s saw a new basis for an improved relationship between the ethnic groups within the Danish Jewish Community on other fronts. First and foremost this was the period during which the administrative procedures within the Jewish Community underwent reform. A group was established whose principal aim was to enlarge the electorate and to ensure proportional voting for minority representatives on the Jewish Community's board. With Abram Krotoschinsky and Pinches Welner as standard-bearers for the reform, the board finally agreed to appoint a committee. In 1933, during C. B. Henriques's leadership of the Jewish Community, changes in the bylaws were adopted which were viewed as reflecting a democratization of the rules of governance that had been in place since 18 February 1849. The old bylaws had been very restrictive on the matter of voter eligibility. The rules were now adjusted in line with those that held for the election of other public councils in the country. There was no longer to be direct election of board members. Instead, the members were to elect an assembly of delegates, whose function would be to act as an electoral college appointing the board of representatives as well as to serve in an advisory capacity. The first meeting of delegates took place in January 1937. The new rules calling for list of nominees drawn from different constituencies turned out to be unnecessary. Instead, there was a single slate—consisting of twenty delegates, five of whom were of "more recent immigrant stock."

C. B. Henriques, in opening the meetings, was thus able to declare that the new set of rules was by no means revolutionary in the Jewish Community's history. "The future will continue to see things done the way they were in the past for more than 100 years," he said, not without a sense of satisfaction. The opposition was also pleased. The spokesman, Abram Krotoschinsky, expressed his thanks to the chairman, adding that the new immigrants had found a well-established, highly respected Jewish Community in Denmark, and they wished only for harmonious continuity of the past into the future. The Eastern European

Jews, curiously enough, chose Binjamin Slor as their representative on the board. He was not born in Eastern Europe but in Petach Tikvah, Palestine. He had come to Denmark as a young atheletics student during World War I and had settled there. He became known for his Zionist activities, and in subsequent years worked tirelessly on behalf of Jews in Palestine, later Israel. Also to be noted in his outstanding job on behalf of young Jewish refugees from Nazi Germany, and his involvement in shaping the Jewish schools in Copenhagen.

If the 1930s nevertheless witnessed strong clashes between the ethnic groups in the Danish Jewish Community, it was not so much a matter of their dissimilar social backgrounds as, above all, their dissimilar response to the events taking place in Germany following the Nazi takeover. It was not that they differed in their willingness to help. Whenever there was a question of going to the official Danish authorities, extending hospitality, or raising funds for the needy, everyone agreed, in principle, to do whatever was possible. There was, however, a clear difference on a psychological level. Those who had experienced anti-Semitism personally knew that it would not simply go away if they maintained a low profile and remained silent. This was a lesson that the others still had to learn. In his book, *Fra polsk jøde til dansk* [*From Polish Jew to Danish Jew*], Pinches Welner gives a most telling account of a meeting in 1933 in Grundtvig's Hus [a public meeting hall], where the question of the fate of Jews in Europe was under public debate. Welner wrote:

> The next official speaker was Attorney Arthur Henriques, secretary of the Jewish Community. Henriques was a kind and lovable human being. But listening to him that night, one could not help but think: If we are destined to lose our lives because we are Jews, it will not be with dignity, but rather in shame. Like an eel, he twisted and turned his argument in order to convince his audience that anti-Semitism could never be caused by *Danish* Jews. Danish Jews were, after all, decent, educated, cultured, and well-mannered people; they were, in other words, beyond reproach. Though not even once did he refer explicitly to Eastern European Jews, his choice of words carried a nasty connotation that left no doubt about his implied meaning. Perhaps he did not recall Göring's revealing comment "When I hear the word 'culture' I reach for my gun."

The people for whom Henriques was the spokesman had apparently not learned anything from the events taking place in Germany.

Welner also recounted an advisory meeting called by the board of representatives in 1933 when Hitler came to power: "The participants gathered quietly as if they were shadows, and then sat equally quietly around the room. They knew how hopeless the situation was." C. B. Henriques [the chairman] proposed that an attempt be made to contact Mussolini in Italy, and through him to try to influence Hitler, but this proposal did not suit Welner:

> We who had participated in the revolutionary movement [in Russia] regarded such humble backstage appeals as humiliating. One should demand one's rights openly in the daylight; one should fight for them. But demanding or fighting was viewed [at the advisory meeting] as impossible. We were after all dealing with a foreign nation where all concepts of humanity had been cast aside, a country which had suspended law and order, and in which brute force ruled. 'No ruler will alter the very policy that brought him to power [I said] and without anti-Semitism the Nazis would not have been able to rally the Germans. The proposed action would be doomed in advance; an intervention might succeed in an isolated instance, but it would not make a dent on the foundation of German politics. We would only court humiliation—and to no conceivable end.' I could readily detect signs of anger on Henriques's face despite his lawyer-like mask of control and somberness; I knew it well from other occasions. His explosions of anger did not occur until I came almost to the end of my speech, at which point he declared: 'You will take to the rostrum time after time, talk endlessly and pass resolutions that are absolutely worthless; to do something real, that you cannot do!' Frankly, he was right. We Eastern Europeans did tend to pass resolutions which we knew beforehand were empty and pointless. It was a kind of game of make-believe power and served to protect our sense of human dignity. The advisory meeting was, in effect, engaged in the same kind of game. The high and mighty gentlemen knew they too were powerless; their outbursts of anger clearly gave them away.

It was only natural that Zionism came to the fore and gained momentum under these circumstances. Here was an ideology which—realistically—would eliminate the shame of being Jewish and helpless. Several Zionist organization were formed, which were active on many fronts. Among the individuals already mentioned, Slor and Welner were strong supporters of Zionism, although they had different perspectives and frequently clashed. But there were many others who supported the Zionist cause. Louis Frænckel, Magna Hartvig, Julius Margolinsky, Josef Nachemsohn, Erik Hertz, Baruch Griegst, Josef Schild, and my own parents, Meta and Marcus Melchior, among many others left their mark on Zionist activities. In some circles the term, "Zionism" remained a dirty word, but when it came to practical assistance in the work of rebuilding Palestine everyone was supportive. And when Chief Rabbi Friediger visited the Holy Land and wrote about it enthusiastically in his book, *Landet der genopbygges* [*The rebuilding of a country*] not an eyebrow was raised.

In October 1938 the Board of Representatives of the Danish Jewish Community took the unusual step of approaching the British government through a communication, which in part read as follows: "There are reports which suggest that the British Government intends to rescind the Balfour Declaration and thus not fulfil its pledge to support the Jewish quest for a national home in Palestine. These reports have caused considerable concern among Jews in Denmark, though we should like to take this opportunity to express our confident belief that you will not [go back on your word]."

When a new situation arose challenging this trust—the publication of the famous British white paper, a document that threatened to set a limit on future Jewish immigration to Palestine—the board of representatives, along with the chief rabbi and the synagogue committee, sent the following resolution dated 7 July, 1939 to the members of the Danish Jewish Community:

> Confident in our belief that the British people, as well as the Mandate Commission in their treatment of the British Government's Palestine proposal will be prepared to reject an unjust solution to a problem so vital to the Jewish people, we will, as Jews, ourselves show our unbending determination to have the re-building of Palestine continue through our constructive efforts, and thereby prevent the *White Paper* from becoming a reality.

Marcus Melchior, who under his initials M. M. wrote a regular feature article in the Jewish Community's monthly publication,

Dr. Marcus Melchior, a brilliant and persuasive figure in the Jewish community and at large, became acting chief rabbi August 1943, filling in for Rabbi Friediger who had been arrested. It was Dr. Melchior who at the special morning service before Rosh Hashanah, on 29 September, warned the congregation of the impending action, urging the more than one hundred members present to spread the word to hide or get away to Sweden. Dr. Melchior served as the refugee's official rabbi in Sweden and upon the death of Dr. Friediger assumed the chief rabbinate of Denmark (1947–1969).

Jødisk Familieblad during that decade, described the resolution as one of the Jewish Community's more "significant documents" and as an "exceedingly wise" one. Of note in the document is the fact that it was not simply an empty letter of protest, one that undoubtedly would have ended up in one of the British government's roomier wastebaskets! Instead, it is an appeal to the membership to demonstrate "not in words but in deeds that Jews themselves have a voice in determining the future of Palestine."

It may well be that Zionism remained a bad word for some people in the Jewish Community, and that in certain Jewish circles it still is today. Yet, that document could not have been more Zionist in spirit and formulation, leaving no doubt as to the solidarity felt by the Danish Jewish Community for the Jews in Palestine and later Israel—a solidarity that is binding. It is thanks to the leaders of the Jewish Community at that time, C. B. Henriques and Karl Lachmann, whose courage, foresight, and, obviously also, willingness to overcome their own personal biases, that the resolution was made possible. The direction of the political course that dated back to 1933 was now finally changed.

The cultural and social activities of the Danish Jewish Community have taken place within an increasing number of clubs and organizations. A few have already been mentioned, but the list is long. In 1912 a Danish branch of B'nai B'rith was formed, a Jewish lodge based upon the motto of "charity, brotherhood and unity." Named "The Denmark Lodge" it was originally a rather exclusive club, consisting of gentlemen who were engaged in supporting many important social welfare services. In the last few decades, the coat-and-tails style of formality has given way to a far more open organization with a broader and more diverse cultural aim and increased struggle against discrimination, but one that still serves welfare needs. Prior to World War II, the women of the Jewish Community could join the Jewish Women's Club, which after the war was transformed into WIZO [Women's International Zionist Organization], an organization in which especially Magna Hartvig and Meta Melchior played leading roles. Thanks to a number of distinguished participants, this Zionist organization eventually grew to become the largest in the Jewish Community—almost one thousand members—whose charge was the support of Israeli kindergartens as well as other cultural and social welfare activities, especially those that pertained to the senior citizens of the Community. The annual WIZO bazaar has become a tradition, drawing some two thousand community members.

The Eastern European immigrants had a knack for getting organizations off the ground. The Jewish Craftsman's Club; a large choir group, Hasomir; and the Jewish People's Club, were among the new organizations in which Yiddish language and culture held sway. For many years there was Yiddish theater, and Hasomir gave annual concerts by its men's and women's choir. Though in the past decade Hasomir has had some difficulty in replenishing its membership, the other organizations continue to be fully active.

In 1924 Hakoah—the athletic association—was founded on the premise of a "sound mind in a sound body." Hakoah has had its major triumphs in the wrestling department with the Kurland brothers, Leiserowitz and Paikin, winning international acclaim. Perhaps equally important was the fact that Hakoah provided the young an opportunity to meet in a pleasant and positive context; allowing them to engage in sports activities and develop friendships at the same time. Like many other organizations, international meets were especially welcome. Hakoah members would gather at the so-called Makkabiads, where Jews from many countries would compete for gold, silver, and bronze medals.

Yet another youth organization deserving of mention is the B'nai Akiva, a religious Zionist organization which has had a great impact on the religious training of our children and young people. When formed in the early 1930s, the organization was the closest Jewish equivalent to the Boy Scouts. Later, its influence was exerted through summer camps for Scandinavian Jews, with many eventually moving to Israel as a function of this earlier inspiration.

Other organizations have come and gone. At one time, for example, there was a Jewish Student Club and the Zionist pioneer groups Hechaluz and Bachad. Other organizations have had more circumscribed goals as their names suggest: the Jewish Bridge Club, the Jewish Chess Club, and the Jewish Bowling Club. The latest wave of immigrants have established the basis for new clubs through their League of Polish Jews in Denmark and Coordinating Committee. In addition there are various fund-raising committees, such as the United Jewish Appeal which is the major fund-raising group for social welfare needs in Israel, and the Jewish National Fund, which along with the task of raising money for trees in Israel, also was responsible for the original "daily nickel in the blue money-box" and the purchase of inscribed certificates and listings in Jerusalem's *Golden Book,* which have supported the fertilization of the soil in Israel for planting trees. Finally, there are the many "friends" committees in support of hospitals, universities, and other institutions—all the members of the Jewish Community occasionally make contributions, as if they were a regular bill to be paid.

While the organizations mentioned above have all been fairly independent of the official Jewish Community, there are those institutions which have some measure of autonomy, yet are closely tied to the Community's administration. The Community's "old-age-pensioner homes," gradually found to be inadequate, might be cited an an example. In the 1960s two modern nursing homes were established in collaboration with the Copenhagen County Authorities. The first home was N. J. Frænckel's Memorial Home in Utterslev. This replaced a small private home in Dyrkøb, founded by N.J. Frænckel. It soon turned out, however, that there was a more substantial need and subsequently, Meyer's Memorial Home, situated behind the synagogue, was remodeled to become a nursing home. This marked a major upgrading of the care provided for the senior citizens of the Community.

While the board of representatives played a leading role in establishing these homes, private initiatives were chiefly responsible for establishing as many as three kindergartens. The first and major one was the kindergarten at the Caroline School. Another was established later serving the needs of the orthodox, while a third was established in Virum, for the convenience of the many young members of the Community who live in the northern suburbs of Copenhagen.

A central component of the Community's life is the Jewish School. Originally two separate schools, the Mosaic Boys' School and Caroline School, they were founded in the beginning of the nineteenth century for the purpose of transforming immigrant children into good Danes. In the first half of the twentieth century, the schools were, in fact, mainly attended by immigrant children. Following the return from Sweden (1945), the schools were merged into a single co-ed school with Harry Pihler as principal. Education-

Several generations of Danish Jews attended the Mosaisk Boys School and the Caroline School for Girls, established in the beginning of the nineteenth century to meet the special needs of Jewish students. Though mostly manned by non-Jewish teachers, it provided not only instruction in Jewish history and religion but a strong sense of cohesion and identity, before moving on to the regular Danish school system after the seventh grade. Seen here is a class in 1939 with the boys school's longtime and dedicated principal Harry Pihler.

ally, the school was considered quite progressive, but it was nevertheless difficult to maintain a high enrollment as the geographical dispersion of the members continuously increased. With the strengthening of the Jewish curriculum a substantial gain in enrollment was achieved in the 1960s and 1970s. Today approximately half of the Community's children attend the school. Its curriculum has achieved an optimal balance between secular and Jewish subjects, a mix that has been attractive to many in the Community.

It is beyond the scope of this article to give anything like a detailed account of the Community's membership or to describe the various features that a numerical breakdown would call for. Suffice it to note that by the beginning of the century there were approximately 3,000 Jews in Denmark. In 1983 the Jewish Community had 2,400 assessed member families, which would roughly correspond to an estimated figure of 6,000 to 7,000 individuals. The number of Jews living in Denmark is, however, somewhat higher than these figures would indicate, in view of a good many resignations from the Jewish Community in recent years as well as suspensions for nonpayment of dues. There is also an additional number of immigrants who have not registered as Jews anywhere. Thus, the total number of Jews in Denmark is more than likely close to 10,000.

The major wave of immigrants has been described earlier in this article, but it should be noted that the Jewish Community is even more pluralistic than that. There are a number of Jews living in Denmark who have immigrated from Israel. Many of these have strong family ties to North African or Asian countries. They have found it rather difficult to integrate into Danish society, since many of them view their stay in Denmark as only temporary, intending eventually to return to Israel. Nevertheless, they have settled in Denmark—family and all—and not least for the sake of their children, they draw on the Community's resources.

Increasing importance must also be assigned to those members who as adults have been converted to Judaism. In some instances such conversions were a consequence of marriage, in other cases knowledge of Judaism has come through other channels. The number of converts varies over time, but the figure is roughly a few hundred. Many of them have proved themselves valuable to the Community, others have been—from a rabbinical point of view—a disappointment. It should be added, however, that to be a proselyte to Judaism is no simple matter. In part this is due to the stringent requirements set by the Jewish faith, and hence by the rabbi, for conversion. But there is also the general skepticism of the native Jew vis-à-vis the convert to contend with. This topic has been the subject of frequent debate, with rabbis being taken to task for their lenience, among certain orthodox groups, whereas others argue for a more accommodating approach.

Divergent views of this kind are unavoidable in a community that attempts to embrace a membership ranging from the strictest orthodox tradition to the more liberal, and even atheistic, position. In an age where large parts of the western world have separate congregations for Orthodox, Conservative, and Reform Judaism, the Danish Jewish Community has successfully maintained a unified character. At the center and as the symbol of this unity is the synagogue [located on Krystalgade], where the services are in accord with all the requirements imposed by rabbinic law, and which, at the same time, has satisfied the aesthetic requirements of the no-less-liberal membership that characterized the nineteenth and twentieth centuries. The congregation has consistently had cantors who were able to live up to exceedingly high standards. In this connection it should be mentioned that the beautiful synagogue building has served as the framework for some of the high points in the community's life during this century. In 1933, commemorating the synagogue's one hundred years' jubilee, His Majesty King Christian X visited the synagogue and was the first Danish monarch to do so. As this visit followed the Nazi takeover in Germany by only a few months, it was correctly perceived as a demonstrative gesture. After World War II, His Majesty King Frederik IX and Her Majesty Queen Ingrid took part on several occasions in ceremonies held in the synagogue, and in 1983 Her Majesty Queen Margrethe and Prince Henrik were present at the celebration of the synagogue's 150 years' jubilee.

Shortly after the turn of the century, Professor David Simonsen resigned his post as chief rabbi. He devoted himself to his priceless library which today is a treasure trove in the Royal Danish Library. Upon the death of Professor Simonsen three decades later, the library established a Judaica section equaled by only a few collections in the world. Professor Simonsen was replaced by Tobias Lewenstein, who had made an enthusiastic impression on the Community leaders by his sermon and his forceful personality. After his appointment his religious bent was found to be more to the right of center than was deemed desirable at the time, so an additional rabbinate was established, with Max Schornstein as its occupant—a turn of events which Tobias Lewenstein rightfully regarded as a violation of the chief rabbi's contract. Some years later this situation led to an open rupture between the chief rabbi and the board of representatives. In 1912 the issue landed in the supreme court with the Community having to pay a hefty fine as well as damages to Tobias Lewenstein.

When Dr. Lewenstein ceased to function as chief rabbi in 1910, a group of his supporters arranged to provide him with his own congregation where he could handle ritual matters autonomously. Thus was formed the organization known as Machasike Hadas. It remained independent, even after Dr. Lewenstein's departure in 1912, and it still exists to this day.

It was thus Chief Rabbi Schornstein who, with the good support of Professor Simonsen, was at the religious helm during the rather hectic period when many immigrants needed to become integrated into the Community. He left Denmark in 1919 and was succeeded by Max Friediger who for twenty-seven years held the chief rabbi's post. It was a period of harmonious collaboration between the religious and the secular leadership. Dr. Friediger was a splendid representative of Jewish traditions. He too availed himself of David Simonsen's knowledge as well as that of Josef Fischer—the official librarian of the Community—whose rabbinical scholarship was considerable. Dr. Friediger was arrested by the Germans on 29 August 1943 and was later deported to Theresienstadt where he made a major contribution looking after the well-being of his fellow prisoners. Shortly after his return he suffered an illness, which led to his death in 1947.

He was succeeded by the Danish-born Rabbi Marcus Melchior, who since his return to Denmark in 1934 [after having served as rabbi in Beuthen, Upper Silesia, 1925–1934] had been active in different capacities in the Community, but only performed rabbinical duties during the refugee period in Sweden (1943–1945). In the subsequent twenty-two years, he was internally, as well as externally, an extraordinary spokesman for the community and enjoyed the reputation of one of the country's best preachers and speakers. It was during this period that the state of Israel became a reality, an event which naturally gave rise to a number of new issues. In this task Marcus Melchior worked in concert with the three personalities who each held the office of chairman of the Jewish Community: Karl Lachmann, Otto Levysohn, and Leo Fischer. It was a collaboration among equals, with ample room for the expression of diverse views.

Since my father's death in 1969, I have held the chief rabbinate. During this period new and severe problems have emerged, such as the plight of the Soviet Jews, and the arrival of a new wave of immigrants. The Community has gone through phases when it

Shortly after the war's end the Danish Jews returned joyfully from their two-year refuge in Sweden to find their homes and jobs waiting for them. The reinvocation of the synagogue in Copenhagen in June 1945, seen here, was a moving event, attended by representatives of the Danish government, church officials, and others from the community at large. Chief Rabbi Max Friediger (left) and Cantor Eugene Goldberger are seen holding the sacred Torah scrolls, which had been kept in safety by the Danes. Dr. Friediger (1884–1947) was one of the 425 Danish Jews who just a few months before had been released from Theresienstadt in an exchange arranged by the Danes and the Swedish Red Cross.

was threatened by internal discord and splits, but these have nevertheless been reversed and a more collaborative spirit established. The best one can say about the bad publicity which resulted from those conflicts is that it showed that the Jewish Community was viewed as a component of Danish society and its internal affairs were treated no differently from those of other components within Danish society at large.

Since 1976 Rabbi Bent Lexner has also been associated with the Danish rabbinate. While my father and I, in earlier years, had the assistance of such rabbinically trained men as Dr. Rafael Edelman and Magister S. Friedman, with Bent Lexner our community has the unique perspective of a rabbi trained in Israel.

The two major events of this century for the Jewish people—the Holocaust and the creation of the state of Israel—have cast a shadow as well as light on the past and the future. The Jews of Denmark have lived through these events; in part they were directly exposed to them—though they were largely saved from the worst consequences—and they were privileged to have had the ability to extend a helping hand to those less fortunate. They were living in a society where the population was not only willing to help them escape the country, but where the really remarkable deed—to quote my father—was the welcome they received upon returning home in 1945. The Jewish Community, for its part has fostered many outstanding women and men who have taken a prideful place in Danish society, whose contributions have left an imprint on the developments in the arts and sciences, in commerce and politics—yes, in all spheres of Danish life. To name them all here would be impossible, but their achievements remain despite their anonymity. Clearly, a substantial segment of the Jews of Denmark has succeeded in combining its sense of Danish community with a genuine commitment to its Jewish heritage along with a feeling of belongingness to the Jewish people.

NOTE

The source material for the quotations in Rabbi Melchior's article come from the archival records maintained by the Danish Jewish Community—unless otherwise noted.

PERSONAL NARRATIVES

4.

Herbert Pundik

The last I remember of Denmark on that October night was the faint sound of the boat cutting through the water as the fisherman poled it away from the shore toward the open sea. It was a good night for escaping from the German coastal patrols. Looking back, I saw two persons kneeling on the sand. One was our host, a friend of my father's, the other was the wife of the fisherman who was going to smuggle us through the German lines from occupied Denmark to neutral Sweden. Their hands were lifted toward heaven. They remained within my sight until the Danish coastline was lost from view.

Once into open water, the fisherman started the motor. Its clunk-clunk tore through the silence. I still remember the search lights from the German patrol boats playing over the dark sky, the silence of the fisherman, who without making any efforts to camouflage his intentions, made a dash for the Swedish coast. I was fifteen, and my curiosity was stronger than my fear of being caught by the Germans.

I counted the minutes. From the time we left Denmark, where Gestapo patrols assisted by some Danish collaborators tried to round up the seven-thousand Jews, to the moment the fisherman called us on deck and told us that we were safe, exactly thirty-seven minutes had passed. A Swedish coastal patrol watched us

First published in *Kings and Citizens: The History of the Jews in Denmark 1622–1983*, vol. 1. New York: The Jewish Museum, 1983. Reprinted by permission of the author and the Jewish Museum.

from a distance, its position marking the line of its territorial waters. The moment we crossed the line the Swedes took over and escorted us into the harbor of Sofiero.

It was the night of 3 October 1943. During that month and the following, about seven-thousand Danish Jews and Jews of foreign nationality living in Denmark were rescued by crossing the sound from Denmark to Sweden. Nearly five-hundred did not reach safety, but were caught by the Gestapo and deported to Theresienstadt, the concentration camp in Czechoslovakia. Approximately fifty died due to sickness and deprivation. The rest returned home after the Nazi defeat, in May 1945.

German forces attacked and occupied Denmark on 9 April 1940. The Danes capitulated almost immediately. Unlike what occurred in most other occupied countries, Hitler allowed the Danes a large measure of independence until 29 August 1943. The government and parliament remained in place. The courts, police, and armed forces continued under Danish jurisdiction. Concessions were made to the occupying power, but by and large Danish society remained intact. Hitler was ready to grant the Danes this wide authority of self-rule as long as they prevented the anti-Nazi underground from getting out of hand, and continued to produce agricultural and industrial products. He saw the Danes as potential partners in his Aryan domain. Hitler also left the Danish Jewish community in peace knowing the Danes would not cooperate if he extended his anti-Jewish policy to Denmark.

While most of European Jewry was being persecuted, deported, and exterminated, the seven-thousand-strong Danish Jewish community continued its life, no less normally than its Gentile neighbors. Protected by Danish police, the synagogues remained open. The Jewish educational system functioned. The Zionist youth organizations continued their activities. With little knowledge of the fate of the rest of European Jewry, most Danish Jews rejected as rumor the snippets of information which reached them.

"It cannot happen here," they said, repeating the slogan of many German Jews before the outbreak of World War II. Those who tried to warn them were scorned and criticized. When Danish newspapers published a German communiqué that denied stories about mass extinction of Jews in Eastern Europe, the majority of the Danish Jews believed it because they so badly wanted it to be true.

Young Danish Jews were advised by the elders of the community against taking part in the anti-Nazi activities of the growing resistance movement. Some of us ignored the advice.

I remember, as a fifteen-year-old schoolboy, getting a dressing down from the Chief Rabbi of Copenhagen, Max Friediger. My parents had discovered that I was involved in distributing illegal anti-Nazi newspapers. When parental persuasion had no effect, the chief rabbi was called in for support. I remember the stern warning, "If you continue your illegal activities you may jeopardize the entire Jewish community." I did not have the moral courage to withstand the chief rabbi's pressure.

The unique situation of Danish Jews came out of a strange collaboration—a Danish government ready to cooperate with the Germans within limits, and a Nazi leadership pretending that Denmark was a kind of ally, and that its occupation was a friendly act. The Danish population, it was thought, would slowly learn to appreciate its privileged position as the German armies went from victory to victory on the mainland.

This illusion was shattered by the events leading up to the final break between the Nazis and the Danish government. Hitler lost the battle of Stalingrad and the German offensive in North Africa collapsed. The Allied forces invaded Italy. The Danish underground movement increased its sabotage activities and clashes took place between Danish civilians and German soldiers. The Germans demanded that the Danish government take stricter measures against the underground movement, and the prime minister offered his resignation. The Germans refused to accept it, hoping that conciliation was still possible.

The chief German representative in Denmark, Dr. Werner Best, was still resisting growing pressure from Berlin to initiate measures against the Danish Jews. On 24 August Dr. Best was called to Berlin for a severe reprimand delivered by his chief, Foreign Minister J. von Ribbentrop, in the name of Hitler.

Best returned to Copenhagen with an ultimatum to the Danish government. He demanded the introduction of emergency laws: strikes were to be prohibited, curfew introduced, acts of sabotage

A young woman wearing a red, white, and blue cap—the Allied emblem—is arrested by a Danish policeman at the behest of a complaining SS officer. The display of pro-Allied sympathies became strictly *verboten* by 1943. Youngsters who had devised a variety of clever and often amusing ways of demonstrating their anti-German feelings—such as wearing tiny little pins with the outlawed colors, misdirecting lost soldiers, pouring sugar into German-owned cars, whistling patriotic songs—were warned by parents and teachers to watch their step.

and possession of arms were to be punished with the death sentence. The government decided to reject the ultimatum and King Christian X supported the position of the political leaders. On 29 August the German forces entered Copenhagen and surrounded the royal residence, Amalienborg. The soldiers and officers of the Danish army were taken prisoner, and the German army declared a state of emergency.

The Danish government resigned and the Parliament went home. The mutual Danish-German conciliation policy which was introduced on the day of occupation, 9 April 1940, could no longer survive the strains caused by the Danish population's growing desire to manifest its anti-German attitude. Leading Danish personalities were taken hostage by the Germans. A general strike ensued. The sabotage activities of the English-influenced underground movement intensified. The fate of the Danish Jewish community was sealed.

Without a Danish government and a cooperative Danish population to please, the Germans saw no reason to continue preferential treatment of the Jews. Immediately after the emergency laws were introduced, they confiscated the lists with names and addresses of the members of the Jewish community. From 29 August 1943, it was only a question of time before the Gestapo would strike. Most Danish Jews woke up to this fact too late. A handful started preparing for escape to Sweden; a few did leave, but the majority believed that danger was not imminent. However, a German ship soon appeared in the Copenhagen harbor, dispatched to deport the Jewish community.

Chief Rabbi Max Friediger had been under arrest since 29 August. On a Friday, the 24 September, a week before the Germans went into action, Werner David Melchior, a leader of the Zionist youth organization and son of the acting chief rabbi, warned his friends by phone to prepare for rescue to Sweden. He called them and said the agreed codeword "*Lekh lekha,*" a quotation from Genesis—"rise and go." Melchior had access to inside information. His warning to his Zionist youth colleagues was simple deduction based on political reality. Melchior was accused by his father, Marcus, of "spoiling Shabbat peace" by issuing his warnings.

The 26 September was a Sunday. It was the seventy-third birthday of King Christian X, the beloved monarch and friend of the Danish Jews.

The synagogue was decorated with flowers and the red and white Danish flag. A special prayer was to be said in honor of the king.

When the sexton of the synagogue asked a leading member of the community "Do you believe we will be able to celebrate Rosh Hashanah as festively as today?" he was told "You are talking irresponsibly. And if you proceed, I shall ensure that you will be refused permission to enter this house."

On Monday, 27 September, Rabbi Marcus Melchior consulted with five of the permanent under secretaries of the central administration who had taken charge in lieu of the cabinet ministers who had resigned on 29 August. They admitted there had been a crisis regarding the future of the Jews, but it had blown over for the time being. They advised the Jews to wait patiently. If anything would happen, the Jews would be properly warned.

Leaders of the Social-Democratic party told their contacts in the Zionist movement that they were following the situation, and would alert them if there were new developments.

That Monday the general impression was that the danger had passed. In the house of the acting chief rabbi, friends gathered to play bridge and have dinner. The Germans had relaxed the curfew from six to nine o'clock in the evening.

On Tuesday the twenty-eighth, the bubble burst. The German commercial naval attaché, G. F. Duckwitz, had on that day warned Hans Hedtoft, the leader of the Social-Democratic party, that a German *Aktion* was under way. According to Duckwitz, 1 October was set as the zero hour. He proved to be correct.

After the war, former Social-Democratic Prime Minister Hans Hedtoft described his meeting with Duckwitz that day.

> I was sitting in a meeting when Duckwitz asked to see me. "The disaster is going to take place," he said. "All details are planned. Your poor fellow citizens are going to be deported to an unknown destination."
>
> Duckwitz's face was white from indignation and shame. . . .
>
> I only replied, "Thanks for the message." Duckwitz disappeared.
>
> I divided the job among some friends. Through an illegal contact with the police we were provided with cars. We went in all directions (to warn the Jews). I chose first to visit the chairman of the Jewish Community, C. B. Henriques, a barrister of the supreme court.
>
> I asked to see him in private. I was upset, nervous and unhappy. "Henriques," I said, "a catastrophe is approaching. The anti-Jewish action, which we all have feared, is on its way. . . . You must immediately take all possible steps to warn every single Jew in town. We shall do our utmost to support you."
>
> Today I can disclose that Henriques reacted differently from what I expected.
>
> He only said two words, "You lie."
>
> It took some effort to persuade him to believe me.
>
> "It can't be true," he said repeatedly, "I don't believe it."

On Wednesday, 29 September, the eve of the Jewish new year, the Jews prepared to go underground. The synagogue was closed the next morning.

Messengers mobilized by the underground movement went from house to house warning the Jews and asking them for information concerning the whereabouts of others. There was no general awareness in Denmark of who was or was not Jewish. Many were surprised to discover that the people next door were Jews, for some Jews had tried so hard to forget their origin that they had nearly succeeded.

A number of Jews took refuge with Gentile friends, and Protestant ministers opened their homes to entire families. Hospitals sent ambulances out on request from the underground to pick up Jews from their homes and transport them to hospitals. There they were registered as patients named Hansen, Jensen, or Petersen and hidden in the wards, the morgues, and the attics. Several were disguised as hospital staff.

There were those Jews who refused to believe that persecution would begin. Descendants of families with ancient lineage, who were Jews by birth but totally assimilated into Danish society, found it especially difficult. They simply refused to face the fact that the Germans had singled them out. Some were actually removed by the underground by force or persuasion while others were caught by the German Gestapo patrols. In one case two elderly ladies went to Dagmarhus, the Gestapo headquarters in Copenhagen, and turned themselves in saying, "We understand that you are looking for Jews?" They were told to go home, pack their bags and return later, which they did. The two ladies were promptly deported to the Theresienstadt concentration camp.

The descendants of more recent Jewish waves of immigration, whose forebears had come from Russia, Poland, and Germany since the turn of the century, were quicker to react to the warnings and go into hiding.

A chief editor of a leading Danish daily was finally persuaded to run for his life by his gentile friends. He went to the coast where the underground had prepared a vessel to take him across the sound to Sweden. But on his way from his hideout to the boat, as he crossed the coastal highway, he was caught by a German patrol.

"What are you doing here in the middle of the night," a German soldier asked him.

"I am trying to escape from you," was his honest reply.

He was arrested but later, through the intervention of influential Danish friends, he was released from German captivity and finally reached Sweden.[1]

I have my own recollection of that Wednesday, 29 September: I was in school when the class was interrupted and the headmaster entered. He pointed at me and a couple of other boys and asked us to join him outside. In the doorway he turned around and said, "Sorry to ask, but are there others in the class of Jewish origin?" The teacher packed his things and joined us in the corridor.

"We have been warned by the underground movement that the German *Aktion* against the Jews is soon to begin," he said. "Please go home and warn your parents."

I was home in ten minutes. There was no time to say goodbye to friends or to pick up some favorite books. The worst, as I recall, was not the fear and feeling of being turned from a carefree schoolboy into a hunted Jew in a matter of hours, but seeing my parents scared and out of control.

An excerpt from a young girl's unpublished diary reads:

> . . . October. Dark nights. Rumors. Fear among those who look different from the others. There is only one sign in the sky. Escape.
>
> . . . It is so difficult to flee. You must leave your home, lock the door behind you, go down the staircase, as you have done thousands of time before. But today it is different. Today you are a refugee. The quiet days, they finished yesterday. When the message came, anxiety rose in your body, replacing the blood in your veins. You go out on the street, watching to see if anyone follows you. Yesterday it would have looked strange, a bit silly. Today your life is at stake.
>
> . . . It was unavoidable. You meet a friend you have not seen for a long while. He greets you warmly, heartily. Invites you for dinner the following evening. . . . You accept the invitation, nod farewell, of course, you will come tomorrow evening.
>
> . . . You reach the railway station. You feel a bit dizzy, a bit insecure. The awareness that you are fleeing returns. It feels intimidating to buy a ticket.

. . . The compartment is getting stuffed slowly with parcels and valises, children and adults. You get affected by an almost festive holiday atmosphere. Whispering and murmuring and an assuring sense of carelessness, light thoughts and ability to forget why you actually are here, in this train, this evening.

. . . And suddenly you realize that these people are on their way, as you are. Grandfathers and grandmothers carrying the little ones while they cradle them in their arms and hum them to sleep. Fathers and mothers, with fear in their eyes, look at playing children, who incessantly want something to eat. Where are the biscuits? Oh, we have forgotten the napkins. Quiet, children, come with me, I shall help you. Quiet, children.

. . . The ticket collector passes. He looks at us with a strange glance in his fair eyes. He does not want to see our tickets. But we have tickets. He passes right through the compartment, with a look on his face, as if he cannot stand the thought of the responsibility he has suddenly been burdened with.

. . . Finally we reach our destination, a small town, at the end of the line, at the open sea, enveloped by endless darkness. Hundreds and hundreds seem to have summoned each other to this place. Unhappy, tortured people. From the small railway station they seep in all directions, cautiously they are being taken into the lowly fishermen's cabins, stuffed together like sheep in their enclosure, ignorant about their fate.

. . . They are in an unknown place, among people who only a few hours earlier were strangers.

. . . The doors to the small rooms are thrust open, everybody is pressed together, more and more are coming. Standing hour by hour, waiting.

. . . Some whisper, others try to silence them. A young girl passes out. An old man collapses. A woman gets pains and starts moaning, everybody hushes and hisses.

(The writer of the diary succeeded in escaping to Sweden, but only after some frightening episodes. The boat scheduled to take her across the sound was discovered and confiscated by the Germans. She had to flee from the fishing village to safety into the nearest wood. The following night the underground movement succeeded in lining up another boat which got through the German lines undetected.)

In the first days after the Gestapo declared war on the Danish

Jews, all was confusion. There was almost no organized effort to save them. The underground movement was as unprepared as the Jews themselves.

The Jews instinctively fled toward the fishermen's villages along the Øresund coast. Many were acquainted with the villagers from summer holidays; others picked up by complete strangers and taken into hiding. Taxi drivers, finding Jews in the streets aimlessly looking for protection, brought them to their homes. Empty summer cottages were broken open so that Jews could be hidden. First hundreds, then thousands of Jews crowded the coastal area, making themselves easy prey for the Gestapo.

Private car owners spent their last drop of rationed gasoline patrolling the hinterland of the coastal area to pick up frightened Jews who had nowhere to go. In the forefront of this action were the leaders of the small coastal communities, the ministers, the physicians, and the teachers.

Before the emergency of 29 August 1943, the Danish police, acting on German orders, had confiscated rowboats and small pleasure crafts from their owners in the coastal area. This was not an action directed against the Jews. It was meant to prevent saboteurs and other underground fighters from escaping to Sweden.

Consequently there was a lack of rowboats which could transport the Jews across the sound. But there was no want of Danes ready to risk their lives and no lack of ideas of how to help the Jews and cheat the Germans.

Little has been published about these first confusing days before the rescue operation was organized. Dr. Jørgen Gersfelt, one of the first to take up the challenge, wrote a book entitled *Saadan Narrede vi Gestapo* (*How We Cheated the Gestapo*), which gives a striking impression of the confusion surrounding the rescue.

Gersfelt organized a rescue operation which saved about 1,100 Jews within a four-week period. In some cases he even accompanied the refugees to Sweden to make sure that infants were drugged in case their crying might alert the Germans.

In the beginning, Gersfelt wrote, the rescue operation was almost playfully easy. Sometimes the fishermen forgot to take any precautions. All seaworthy motorboats plied the waters between Snekkersten village and the Swedish coast. Carrying children in their arms and dragging heavy valises, Jews arrived by car and

Dr. Jørgen Gersfelt, the physician in Rungsted who helped Sam Besekow (see p. 130) and some 1100 other Jews across the sound. His name—along with those of Bertelsen, Ege, Staffeldt, Kieler, Borchsenius, Lillelund, Kiær, Rønne, Bruhn, Helweg, Stærmose, Kalby, and literally thousands of others who took part in the rescue effort—ought to be recorded for posterity. Not to be forgotten are the Jewish helpers—among them the names of David Sompolinsky, Erich Marx, Uri Yaari and Ina Haxen stand out, though the list could be expanded.

train. In broad daylight, they swarmed into the ports, and boarded the boats that waited for them with their motors running. The busy scene at the harbor reminded Gersfelt of a vacation spot on a Sunday, when the crowds were returning home from a picnic in the woods.

For thirty-six hours all went well, Gersfelt recounted. Then the

Gestapo appeared in the harbor and began arresting the crews as they returned in their boats.

However, during the first phase of the rescue, the Gestapo was understaffed. Its unit in Elsinore, the main town of the rescue area, had problems in preventing the transports. The German army was called in to help. But the soldiers were not enthusiastic about the *Aktion*. Some, according to Gersfelt, were openly against it.

He cited an instance when a German army patrol stopped a garbage truck in which Jews were hiding. The soldiers lifted the lid and saw them. "Abraham, Isaac, and Jacob," one of them exclaimed and dropped the lid down, gesturing the truckdriver to continue.

Sometimes forty to fifty people took refuge in his house, Gersfelt recalled. "One would think that I was a famous healer, not a young, recently graduated physician."

Some of his "guests" had received his name from other Jews; some had been handed a piece of paper with his address on it by strangers. His home became a clearing house from which Jews were assigned to other places. Fishermen contacted him to tell him when they were ready to ferry Jews to Sweden. Gersfelt and his wife kept lists of Jews looking for boats, and fishermen who were looking for passengers. When morning arrived, passage had been secured for all the Jews, even for those who could not pay.

Many Jews had not reached the coast in time. As the days passed the Gestapo received reinforcements. Fearing discovery, some Jews went so deeply into hiding that they lost contact with their potential rescuers. But fortunately, Gentile friends and members of the resistance spared no effort to find them and get them out of the country.

My own family's story is a case in point. Our first attempt to organize passage to Sweden failed. We were waiting in a large private villa situated on a cliff overlooking the beach. We had no details about the rescue. None of us realized until later that almost ninety-five percent of the Danish Jews would be saved. We only knew that we were in danger of being caught and deported by the Gestapo.

It was 2 October, the second day of the *Aktion,* and we waited with others for one of the rowboats that ferried Jews to Sweden about ten miles away. Due to the Gestapo's increased activities, the fishing harbors were now out of bounds, and the rescue was to take place from isolated points along the coast.

When our turn came, the organizer, his face white with tension, said, "No more tonight."

The fisherman who had just rowed back from a tour across the sound entered the room. He raised his hands in a gesture of defeat. His palms were torn to shreds—bloodied—from the rowing effort.

Under cover of darkness we were quickly smuggled back to one of the fishermen's cottages further inland and told to wait for another opportunity.

One day passed with no message. The German patrols had been intensified. They were bringing dogs. A Danish informer and traitor in the vicinity was searching for Jews, offering money for information concerning our whereabouts. Whenever a stranger approached the cottage, we hid in the cupboards, under the beds, and in the attic.

Once the doorbell rang. The fisherman opened it. A voice asked, "Have you heard about a family Pundik? They were last reported heading for this village."

Our host denied any knowledge of the family. The stranger persisted, suggesting that the Pundiks were hiding with neighbors. Once again, our host feigned ignorance.

Then I remember my father crying out, "We are here, we are here!"

The stranger rushed into the house. He was an old business acquaintance of my father who lived about twenty miles further north along the coast. Mr. Nicolaisen, an elderly man, who needed the support of a cane, had walked twenty miles from the village of Aalsgaarde to Humlebæk, our hiding place. He had knocked at the doors of all the houses situated along the coastal road, asking the inhabitants for information about our family.

Hoping to find us, Mr. Nicolaisen had organized our passage in advance. A private automobile, burning wood for fuel, soon arrived, and through the narrow roads along the farmland behind the coast, we reached the Nicolaisen villa. That same night a fishing boat picked us up from the coast adjoining the villa.

An hour later a Swedish patrol boat escorted us into a Swedish harbor. Our Danish fisherman waved goodbye and turned back to the darkened Danish coast, which had been completely blacked out for three years, since the German occupation of Denmark began in 1940.

Seven thousand human beings—Jews—were rescued during October and November of 1943. It was a remarkable event, made up of many individual acts of courage, as well as astounding group initiative. The Danish physicians were one of the professional groups most actively involved in the rescue operations.

In a book entitled *Den hvide Brigade: Danske Lægers Modstand* (*The White Brigade: The Resistance of Danish Physicians*) Dr. Steffen Lund described how the municipal hospital of Copenhagen, *Kommunehospitalet,* prepared to go to the assistance of the Jews. The whole hospital staff, one thousand people, were involved in the rescue. The leaders assumed that the anonymity of such a large group would protect them against German punitive measures.

"We also needed much assistance in contacting Jews in their homes and searching for them in their hiding places," wrote Dr. Lund.

> We soon realized that some Jews had left their homes with nowhere to turn. Some were hiding in the municipal parks, especially the one facing our hospital. During the nights, they entered the hospital and asked for food.
>
> When we realized this, we called a meeting with the practicing physicians, one from each district of Copenhagen. They knew their patients trusted them. They could look up their Jewish patients, they could ask neighbors where they were. Everybody would be pleased to reply to their questions. The assembled physicians could again contact their colleagues. Thus, in a short time, the message quickly apread all over town, that Jews should turn to the hospitals for help. From here they would be transported to Sweden. That is how we started the ingathering of the Jews.
>
> Many Jews had also gone into hiding in the wooded countryside. Through one of our medical chiefs we established contact with a voluntary organization called the Academic Rifle Club. They put a group of cross-country runners at our disposal. They were well disciplined and knew both to take orders and act independently. In a short while, two hundred of them had searched through the for-

ests which they knew like the back of their hand. Many Jews were picked up in this manner. In one forest they found thirteen Jews who had been hiding for one week, surviving on turnips, which they stole from the fields during the night.

The physicians' rescue work was coordinated by a central command which met every day. It never met in the same place twice and it moved from one hospital in Copenhagen to another. The network was financed first by private contributions, later as the activities grew, large funds, sometimes hundreds of thousands of kroner (read U.S. dollars in today's value) were required. Many of the Jews rescued by the physicians' organization were poor, and could not finance their own transport to Sweden. The group saved about 2,000 Jews during the weeks of October and November, 1943.

The cost of saving a Jew varied in the first days of the *Aktion*. However, life was at stake and money had lost its value. Prices were highest at the outset, when the rescue operation was chaotic. Eventually, the underground movement got control of the rescue routes and ousted the middlemen and profiteers who tried to exploit the fear and confusion of Jews ready to pay anything to reach safety. Some fishermen charged money to ferry Jews to Sweden, others only took money from those who could afford it. A few wealthy Jews financed the passage of those who could not pay.

Prices for a person varied from one-thousand to about ten-thousand kroner. But no Jew was left stranded for lack of money or contacts with the rescue operation. As it grew, the underground movement began financing passages. Leaders of the rescue work made contact with people of means who donated large sums of money to finance part of the costs. In several cases the organizers not only risked their lives collecting, hiding, and escorting the Jews, but they also personally guaranteed some of the private loans taken to help fund the costs. Sometimes people mortgaged their homes to finance the operations.

Most money went for paying the fishermen and buying the boats. After the opening phase of the rescue operation the underground began buying larger boats, up to twenty tons, taking big groups of refugees in one sweep across the sound.

Bribery was rarely necessary. In most cases the Danish harbor police, which formally controlled the small ports, and the Danish general police, which patrolled the coastal area, cooperated with the rescuers. In a couple of instances some of the younger policemen complied too strictly with their instructions. They were quickly taught a different lesson by their officers.

On one occasion, some young policemen arrested a group of Jews and prepared to take them to Elsinore for detention. The underground contacted their superior who rushed to the scene, piled the Jews into his car, and drove them to a safer location. On another occasion the underground had to use threats of force when a young harbor policeman tried to prevent a group of Jews from boarding a boat he was guarding. He acquiesced to the underground's demands after they showed him a couple of pistols.

In addition, the Germans were not very efficient. As mentioned earlier, the German army and navy were, in this case, not too helpful to the Gestapo. Leni Yahil wrote in her work about the Jews in Denmark during the occupation, that it seemed "that there hardly was one German left in Denmark who was prepared to execute the action against the Jews along the lines followed in others places." Even after the reinforcement had arrived, the Gestapo stationed in the coastal area was understaffed. Furthermore, according to the reports of surviving leaders of the rescue operation, the Danish-speaking German Gestapo chief in Elsinore, "*Gestapo-Juhl*" as he was called, was something of a bungler.

There was one more crucial element, the Danes were more daring than the Germans had expected. For instance, in Elsinore harbor the rescue boats operated right under the noses of the Germans. On another occasion, the underground broke into empty German freight cars parked on the regular ferry going from Elsinore to Sweden to pick up goods destined for Germany. Jews were placed in these freight cars, which were then closed with the original German seal that the underground had somehow obtained. This escape route, particularly suited for the old and the very young who could not withstand the hardships of a rough autumn sea passage, was unfortunately discovered. Once safely in Sweden, a few of the human "freight" chattered too much and the secret was reported in a Swedish newspaper. The result was that until the ferry left Elsinore for Helsingborg on the other side of the sound, the freight cars remained under the watchful eyes of German guards.

How was the rescue perceived from the neutral Swedish side? Here is an eyewitness account from a Swedish newspaper article from October 1943:

> . . . We are standing on the beach, watching the dark water. Milk white fog was mercifully clouding the surface of the sea, but the moon, green from fear, was shining in the sky. We were waiting for hours, the cold of the night was enveloping our feet. Will anybody cross tonight, some poor refugees . . . will they escape the hunt taking place on the other side?
>
> The excitement is growing. You believe you hear the sound of oars hitting the water, you see masts appearing from the darkness. But it is your imagination playing. On such a night you want so much to see and hear.
>
> And suddenly you hear a throbbing from somewhere, the sound of a motor. Clunk-clunk. Your heart beats through your clothes, competing with the sound from the darkness. The bow of a ship appears through the fog. People are crowding the deck, packed like sardines, hanging in clusters over the rail of the ship.
>
> Slowly the boat approaches, the pale faces of the passengers are all directed towards the entrance to the harbor. They look like ghosts without bodies. The darkness envelops all but their white upturned, . . . expressive faces, some petrified, some displaying suffering, and some radiant with happiness. But on the faces of all of them you read fatigue, a bottomless feeling of fatigue and resignation coupled with the traces of the fear and excitement just experienced.
>
> And suddenly the tension is relieved. Someone on board starts singing "Du gamla, du fria" (the Swedish national anthem). And everybody joins, as best as they know. They remember a word here or there of the text, but nevertheless, bright happy voices join in a mighty chorus.
>
> It is almost more than you can bear. Tears run down the cheeks of tall, hefty men standing on the beach, watching. Here they come, hunted from home and house, driven from their jobs and sometimes torn away from relatives, and here they come, singing, as if they were approaching the gates of Paradise, from death to life.
>
> The boat draws alongside the quay. A Swedish officer calls out a hearty "welcome." The refugees hurry on land with their small bundles. Many fight to keep back their tears, their reactions are overwhelming. A Jew kneels and kisses the soil of Sweden. It is no theatrical gesture. That is what he feels in this very moment. Swed-

ish soil has become holy soil for those who were hunted like animals and had to flee for their lives.

The Germans in Denmark bungled the action against the Jews. The main reason they did not succeed was the fact that they were facing an almost united front of Danes, who refused to remain passive at a moment when their Jewish fellow citizens were in deadly danger. The Danes formed a human wall of daring and silence around the rescue operation. Only a few informers succeeded in penetrating the organization, although a large part of its activities were conducted in broad daylight and lots of people were privy to its secrets. The majority were people without any experience in conspiratory or clandestine work.

The October rescue action became a dramatic turning point in the history of Danish resistance against the German occupiers. After more than three years of occupation a large part of the Danish population was ripe for action. The emergency laws promulgated by the Germans on 29 August 1943, and the resignation of the Danish government removed the last illusion Danes might have harbored—that their war would be different from all other occupied nations' wars. The unavoidable consequence of the 29 August was the introduction of anti-Jewish measures on the first of October. This provocation became the spark that ignited the majority of the Danes to action, turning the resistance movement from a band of the few and daring into an organization with broad popular support. A large part of the people who volunteered for the rescue effort remained in the underground, becoming saboteurs or members of groups producing and distributing the many illegal newspapers. Others provided hospitality for allied airmen shot down over Denmark and for Danish agents who had to live underground and change addresses continuously to avoid German discovery.

The Danes saved the Jews. And this, in turn, contributed to saving the self-respect of the Danes. After 1 October, the resistance grew in scope and activity. The Danes earned the compliments of Field Marshal Montgomery, who called the Danish resistance movement "second to none." Thanks to the underground movement Denmark became recognized as a member of the group of allied nations defeating Nazi Germany.

Most of the Danish Jews had reached safety by the end of November 1943. Only a few trickled across the sound during the following months: elderly people from the Copenhagen area who had been difficult to move, small children who were left by their parents with Gentile friends or relations for safekeeping, and Jews from the provinces who had difficulties in reaching the rescue area in time.

By April 1945, 7,220 Danish Jews and so-called half-Jews and 686 Gentile spouses were registered in Sweden.

But this fortunate story, one of the few bright spots in the history of the Holocaust, also had its dark side. A small number of Jews set out for the Swedish coast but never reached safety. Their rowboats and kayaks capsized on the way due to bad weather or bad seamanship. Some were intercepted by German patrol boats. A few people committed suicide.

But most of the 464 Jews the Germans succeeded in detaining were caught on land, before they reached the rescue boats. In most cases the arrests were due to information provided by Danish agents serving the Nazis. Baruch Griegst and Arie Griegst, father and son, escaped deportation by a stroke of good fortune. They were on their way to a harbor outside Copenhagen, where a large boat was waiting for a consignment of Jews. Their bus had a flat tire on the way, and when it finally arrived at its destination the boat had already sailed. It was caught on the sound by German patrol boats and the Jews on board were later deported in cattle cars to Theresienstadt.

Some of the Danish rescuers were arrested by the Germans and confined to prison. A few were deported to concentration camps in Germany, and some never returned to Denmark.

The Germans caught only seven percent of the Danish Jewish population. They were all deported to Theresienstadt, a concentration camp in occupied Czechoslovakia, where fifty-two of them died of disease and deprivation. From November 1943 on, Danish authorities succeeded in persuading the Germans to permit the supply of some food and medicine to the imprisoned Danish Jews. The Germans refrained from deporting Danish Jews to the extermination camps further east. This was decided during a meeting between Dr. Werner Best and Adolf Eichmann which took place in Copenhagen on 2 November 1943. Danish authorities made this request to Best, who supported the idea. So did, apparently, Foreign Minister von Ribbentrop.

In June 1944, the Jews in Theresienstadt were visited by a Danish delegation consisting of a representative of the Danish Foreign Office and one from the Board of Health.

The Germans, intent on creating the impression that Theresienstadt was a kind of recreation camp for detained Jews, put on a grand show. The part of the camp where the Danes were imprisoned was cleaned up and painted. The prisoners were given new clothes. Threatened with punishment if they failed to take part in this German charade, the prisoners were coached in what to reply to the Danish visitors. the kindergarten was painted and renovated; flowers were planted. Because they looked the most fit, the newest arrivals among the children were selected to receive the Danish delegation. They were instructed to say, when the delegation entered "Oh, we're going to have sardine sandwiches again today."

This incident warrants a longer and more detailed description. Suffice it to say that the visit failed to convince the Danish delegation, but it did encourage the Jewish inmates. Particularly encouraging were the greetings from King Christian. His message was conveyed by the delegate from the Danish foreign ministry, who whispered to one of the Danish Jews "I am delivering the most sincere regards from the king. He is with you in his thoughts."

Nearly ten months passed between the Danish delegation's visit and 13 April 1945, which began like any other day in Theresienstadt. Ralph Oppenhejm, Danish writer and journalist, recorded in his diary: "Grey and endless, like hundreds of other days have started here. . . . The door was torn open, and Mrs. Hald came rushing in, her face pale, her body trembling with excitement.

" 'We are leaving for Sweden, we are leaving for Sweden.'

"Tears streamed down her face. 'It is true, for Sweden.' And she disappeared."

Melanie Oppenhejm related in another memoire how the Danish Jews were ordered into the basement of one of the barracks of the concentration camp. There they were kept for several days. One day an inmate observed a white bus with Swedish license plates.

Mrs. Oppenhejm writes how relieved they all were at the prospect of evacuation, yet how overcome they were with worry and concern over the fate of the other Jews who would be left behind in the hands of the SS.

The Germans counted the 425 Danish Jews (some 50 had died, primary those in the above 60 age group) for the last time, and handed them over to a representative of the Danish Red Cross. The rescuers were in a hurry. Allied planes were bombing the area around Dresden, through which the convoy of white buses planned to pass.

The convoy stopped at Padborg, the Danish town across the German-Danish border. The Danish population received the Jews with flowers and invited them home for a shower, their first since they had been deported in October 1943. People brought the rescued Jews open sandwiches—real food.

When the white convoy passed through the island of Funen, the Germans sounded an air-raid alert, forcing people into the shelters so no one would see the buses passing. The journey did not end in Copenhagen, but in Malmö, the southernmost part of Sweden.

The detained Jews had finally reached the safety of Sweden, one year and seven months later than their friends and relatives who had succeeded in escaping during the great rescue of October 1943.

NOTE

1. See chapter 5 for Valdemar Koppel's complete story.

REFERENCES

Gersfelt, Jørgen. *Saaden narrede vi Gestapo*. Copenhagen: Gyldendal, 1945. (Not available in English.)

Svendstorp, Aage, ed. *Den hvide Brigade: Danske Lægers Modstand*. Copenhagen: Carl Allers, 1946. (Not available in English.)

Oppenhejm, Ralph. *Det skulle saa være*. Copenhagen: H. Hirschsprung, 1945. (Not available in English.)

Oppenhejm, Melanie. *Menneskefælden*. Copenhagen: Hans Reitzel, 1980. (Not available in English.)

Yahill, Leni. *The Rescue of Danish Jewry: Test of a Democracy*. Philadelphia: Jewish Publication Society of America, 1969.

Valdemar Koppel (1867–1949) was a venerable newspaperman in Denmark. He served as editor in chief of *Politiken* between 1933 and 1937. He describes his escape attempts with typical Danish humor.

5.

Valdemar Koppel

I do not tend toward megalomania and do not for a minute fool myself into thinking that the small amount of stress I suffered at the hands of the Germans is anything compared to what millions of others were subjected to—if anything, I am almost ashamed that it turned out to be so relatively insignificant.

And yet, the story of my experiences might serve to give people who were not involved an idea of what actually happened, what a manhunt in the mid-twentieth century was like. Also I have another motive for telling my story—I don't so much want to get even with anybody as I simply wish to express my gratitude for the goodness, compassion, and helpfulness with which I and my fellow refugees were met during those difficult days, often from a totally unexpected source. None of us will ever forget the help and support we received.

MY FIRST ATTEMPT TO ESCAPE VIA HUMLEBÆK TO THE SWEDISH COAST

Monday, 4 October 1943, in the late afternoon when darkness had already fallen, my wife and I were sitting dejected and nervous on a bench in the small train station of Klampenborg,[1] hoping that we would be able to board the train passing through from Copen-

First published in *Politiken*'s *Magasinet,* 1945. Reprinted by permission. Translated by Ida Pagh (with the assistance of Leo Goldberger). Editor's interpolations appear in brackets and in Notes.

hagen and get unseen and unhurt to Humlebæk on the north coast of Zealand. During the previous eight to ten days we had been fugitives, not daring to remain in our home and staying apart in various places. Eventually we had been told that we had a chance to flee to Sweden on a boat from Humlebæk, so we had hastily scraped together a little luggage and had taken a cab to Klampenborg Station—avoiding the central station in Copenhagen which, so the rumor said, was infested with Gestapo agents on the look-out for refugees. Here in Klampenborg we were supposed to meet with our son, who had just been released from a totally undeserved sojourn in Vestre Prison's German-controlled block, and his family. (On 29 August that same year he had been arrested for a second time under suspicion of having permitted the basement in his villa to be used for the criminal purpose of editing and printing illegal publications. Accordingly he had languished for a month in prison, while it never occurred to the clever Germans that the criminal activities of which he was suspected had been going on in the basement of the neighbouring, absolutely identical villa!)

Here we were then, every minute dragging on for eternities, in the blacked-out station whose total darkness somehow imparted a sense of security. Suddenly we heard the clear, high-pitched voice of a child declaring in happy and uninhibited tones, "We're going away to live in another place!" We recognized the voice as belonging to our small, three-year-old grandchild, Karen. Like so many other children who were fleeing during those days Karen had been given a sedative but the initial effects of the drug were the opposite of the usual ones, and therefore the child became excited and resisted all attempts to persuade her to be quiet. The same phenomenon was seen with quite a few other refugee children. At any rate, the declaration was not too felicitous, but luck would have it that no Gestapo men were present in Klampenborg Station.

NO "BLOOD MONEY"

The train arrived, laden with Jewish refugees who tried to be inconspicuous with their heavy luggage in unlit corners. In Humlebæk Station we were met by a stranger who led us along an interminably long road to the small sitting room of a fisherman's cottage. Sitting at a table underneath a garish paraffin lamp we met a broad-shouldered, elderly fisherman with whom we now had to negotiate the price for the passage across the sound to Sweden.

Having at first declared that he and his mates did not want to receive "blood money" (his own words), he eventually after some hesitation came round to 12,000 kroner as the going price for the five of us, my wife and I, my son and daughter-in-law and the child. Before taking our departure we had scrambled together all available money, but, after all, 12,000 kroner! A counteroffer, issued in a subdued voice, resulted in the sum's being reduced to 10,500 kroner; 10,000 for the passage money and 500 for a consolation prize for the fisherman's wife, who would have to sit in anguish while the husband set out on this trip, which, indeed, represented a certain personal risk to himself.

Generally, the payments asked by the fisherman were not exhorbitant—an average payment of 2,000 kroner per person for a passage across the sound was quite usual in those days. Wealthy Jews paid up to 4,000 to 5,000 kroner and examples were cited of even larger sums, of 40,000 and even 50,000 kroner. One should bear in mind the heavy risks run by the fishermen—prison and confiscation of their boats and tackle, not to speak of the risk of being shot at and sunk. That very same night eight fishing boats loaded to the brim with refugees departed for Sweden from Snekkersten, [a small village between Humlebæk and Elsinore] but all the fishermen were arrested upon their return and imprisoned in Horserød prison camp where they received rather brutal and harsh treatment. I saw them myself there, a magnificent bunch, among them young and vigorous men who refused to lose heart, but we, the others in the camp, were strictly forbidden to have anything to do with them.

At this juncture I ought to mention the persistent rumors which I am personally unable either to affirm or deny, that the fishermen in some instances gave free passage to impecunious Jewish refugees, and that in other cases the fisherman, once he had obtained what he had stipulated as the price—say 50,000 kroner—accepted additional passengers without payment. In any case, these were days when one or five hundred kroner bills were flying through the air, landing almost everywhere. What was the value of money when it came to saving one's life and to live with dignity away from the Gestapo's clutches?

So it was with a calm mind that I counted up the 10,500 kroner, while a shimmer of gold, which certainly did not stem from the paraffin lamp, spread across the small, low-ceilinged room of the fisherman.

CAPTURED!

In heavy rains, gale, and darkness, almost fumbling along, we left, not in the direction of Humlebæk Harbor, which was feared to be under surveillance by the Germans, but toward the nearby hamlet, Sletten, where the boat was supposed to be moored in a presumably safe place.

I was walking furthest behind with a young student from Copenhagen, who had been involved in organizing the flight, and a fisherman, the latter pulling a bicycle, loaded with the heavily crammed haversack which held the belongings of one of us.

Our party was an easy prey—one German car passed without noticing us—we all dived behind trees or nearby walls—but shortly afterward a second car arrived; perhaps the same one as before which, having lost its way, was now coming back. This car spelled my fate.

The fisherman next to us shouted, "Into the garden" and disappeared, crashing his way into a thicket. Only the student remained behind, trying to assist me, as I was fumbling helplessly around, blinded by the headlights of the approaching car which now slowly came to a halt right in front of us. There's no need to elaborate, I was the Gestapo's prisoner!

I have later heard various versions of my capture, one of them was that when I was asked by one of the two Gestapo men, "What are you doing here?", I was supposed to have retorted, "I am trying to escape from *you!*" The remark sounds funny. But those were not the words spoken. Nevertheless, it is true that at the spur of the moment I was incapable of giving any reasonable explanation of what I was doing there on the road in the middle of the night. There was not much point in playing games. My student companion however, does not recall my having made any such or similar remark but an altogether different one, which I have also forgotten: As prisoners in the car on our way to the police station in Elsinore, one of the Gestapo men suddenly shone his flashlight right into my face, asking, "*Sind Sie Jude?*", whereupon I answered, "*Gewiss, und Sie?*" ["Are you Jewish?" "Certainly, and You?"] This repartee caused the Gestapo man to sink back into his corner of the car, horrified by the very thought of belonging to that race.

Incidentally, the two Gestapo men who had captured my companion and me were not the worst sort; you could talk to them. During the drive to Elsinore one of them told me that it was sheer idiocy of me to flee if—as I had said—I was married to an Aryan, since no one would touch me. He asked me whether anyone had been trying to pick me up at my home, and as I could only reply that to my knowledge this was not the case, he almost triumphantly remarked, "*Nah, sehen Sie!*" ["So there, you see?"] It would seem that he was well informed about the limits of the manhunt—criteria that held for the time being, at least, but which had not authoritatively been made public. He then asked me where my wife was, and as I could not very well tell him that at this moment she probably was on the beach waiting for a boat to Sweden, I said I didn't know. This suspicious reply, taken in conjunction with the fact that neither the student nor I carried any identification papers (my streetcar season pass did not qualify), led to our being taken back to Copenhagen in the middle of the night, after the preliminary interrogation at the Elsinore police station, first to Gestapo headquarters, Dagmarhus, and then to Vestre Prison. I still have vivid recollections of the station house in Elsinore, of a lively discussion between the student and the Gestapo man. The student heatedly reproached the German for the assault on Denmark on 9 April 1940 and Germany's blatant violation of the Non-Agression Pact, while the German tried as well as he could to defend himself, arguing that the reich was the only state that was sacrificing its lifeblood for a new Europe. He knew Göbbels's phrases by heart.

IN DAGMARHUS AND VESTRE PRISON

Dagmarhus at night was not an inviting place. The rooms were dimly lit by single bulbs here and there, and there were Germans spread about, sleeping on sofas and cots. But Vestre Prison was worse. This was where the student and I parted company at 3:30 a.m., being led to separate cells. The student, I was later told, was to spend four to five days in solitary confinement, the only reading matter being an old copy of the weekly paper, *B. T.*—which he eventually learned by heart, passing a memory test of his own devising. He was then released—that is, the German police formally handed him over to the Danish police—and driven to the main police station where he was received with cheers, coffee, and cigarettes.

Things turned out somewhat differently for me. My stay in prison did in fact not exceed twelve hours, but that was enough for me. First of all my pockets and luggage were searched. My luggage consisted of only my wife's bag, the haversack having gone astray somewhere along the line (I was to get it back two years later), but I had somehow managed to salvage this bag with its jumbled contents, through all the vicissitudes of those days. Besides my wife's things there were to be found our travel funds, now lightened after Humlebæk to six to seven thousand kroner, all in ten-kroner bills and hidden by her fur cape. The guard conducting the search started counting the money but soon grew impatient and exclaimed, "My God, Man, what are you doing with all that money?" I gave the evasive reply that it was rather nice to have a bit of money on hand, these days you never knew. Well, he resumed his counting but didn't really get anywhere and in the end he simply shoved all the money back into the bag, which he then returned to me, having confiscated only my nail file and pocketknife. Then he left and turned off the light.

Vestre Prison was a disgusting place, but as it already has been described by others, I will not go into much detail. In the morning I was given a stack of stale chunks of rye bread and a plate of unappetizing ersatz honey which I didn't touch. The guards were humane enough though their shouting was awfully loud. When I asked one of them, "Why do you shout so loud?", he looked surprised at me. This was the way it was supposed to be. Everything was to be "*Tempo, Tempo!*" "*Schneller, schneller!*" was the command yelled at me both as I went out to empty the stinking chamber pot and as I went up the stairs after a walk in the prison yard. "*Schneller, schneller!*" However, when I protested that I could not go any "*schneller,*" they did leave me in peace and one of them, the guard on duty on the second floor, even got up to let me sit and catch my breath while the other prisoners were passing. I had not had a haircut for several months; perhaps my dignified white curls over the ears and in the nape of the neck had done the trick—unfortunately not two hours later.

In my wife's bag there was also a pack of cards and I had just settled down to my favorite game of solitaire after the walk, when I was suddenly told to pack my belongings and come along. At the same time my nail file and knife were returned to me. The only thing I had lost so far was a small vial of poison which I had been carrying with me all the time—as did most other Jews in that period just in case—one of the Gestapo men had taken it from me in Elsinore.

GERMAN CULTURE AND THE TREATMENT OF PRISONERS

Things were obviously about to happen. The following events, however, are a bit vague in my memory. One thing I do know is that it became clear to me that I was going to join a small group of other prisoners, all seemingly Jewish in appearance, and I was seized with a very understandable fear that we were to be deported to either Germany or Poland. I had of course heard the rumors of the three ships waiting in readiness in Copenhagen's Langelinie harbor. I therefore took the liberty of addressing a Gestapo man alerting him to the fact that a misunderstanding must have occurred in my case. As the husband of an Aryan, I ought to be released. The man listened to me but did not make a response. We prisoners were led to a corridor and were ordered to stand, face to the wall, and not to move.

But now I had decided I was going to see what was taking place and stole a glance away from the wall. After all, I am a journalist! Among those I saw standing in the line were some elderly ladies, among them the eminent Miss Hanna Adler, founder and school principal of the Sortedam Grammar School; despite her eighty-four years, she stood erect as a queen as she faced the wall. There were several other people, a lady with a bad leg holding on to a cane; a young mother with a whimpering infant on her arm. A group of officers were sitting at a table a small distance away. A number of male and female staff members were moving back and forth, one of them brought a bottle of milk to the young mother.

I made up my mind to make one more attempt and turning round explained that a mistake was being made in my case. But instantly a furious Gestapo man, a fat little fellow, flew at me, and turned me back toward the wall. As I went on protesting, he managed almost simultaneously to kick me in the behind and give me a resounding whack on the ear, a blow that made my head ring; I could feel it even the next day. By now I had gotten good and mad! "To hit a man of seventy-six," I screamed, "I have never experienced anything like it!" "*Sie werden vieles noch schlimmeres erleben!*" ["You will experience far worse things!"] the bully shouted as he grabbed me by the neck from behind and violently and repeatedly banged my head against the wall. Luckily my hat absorbed some of the blows, otherwise I would have had a concussion. During this burst of violence the other Jewish prisoners stood petrified like graven images while the German officers and other administrative staff members seemed in no way affected; for them, perhaps, this was a daily occurence not worthy of note. A remarkable thing did occur, however. After first being locked up for a while in a room and then once more being ordered to stand at attention in the corridor, a chair was brought for the lady with the stiff leg and to my great astonishment I heard a voice behind me saying, "*Geben sie auch dem alten Mann einen Stuhl.*" [Give the old man a stool too.] Based on the episode one would have to conclude that the Germans were not all of one mind when it came to the ways they should treat innocent prisoners.

I was given a chair.

Then came the moment when we were all ordered to mount one of the big transport trucks parked in the yard. It was one of the "prairie wagon" types, familiar to everyone from the streets during the German occupation, with no ladder or running board; one had to climb up with the help of a rope hanging down. I didn't manage too well, but up I got in the end. Miss Adler, on the other hand, got up with no apparent trouble as if she were the gymnastics instructor of her school.

DRIVING TO HORSERØD IN THE PRAIRIE WAGON

The mood on board the truck was at first very dejected, but things livened up quickly as we felt more and more convinced that we were not headed for the harbor. We overheard the orders "Hillerød" and "Horserød," destinations that were incomparably more promising than deportation to a concentration camp in Germany. The weather was lovely and sunny and as we were leaving the city we could enjoy the view from under the canvas top. Unfortunately the drive turned out to take rather long, some three and a half hours, because the driver did not know where he was. He had absolutely no idea about the location of Horserød. Nor did his friends who were guarding us, loaded guns in hand. It was the prisoners who eventually had to take over and direct the driver in the right direction. A rather comic situation. And thus, at last, after many detours and wrong turns we arrived in Horserød, Tuesday, 5 October, at around five o'clock.

I would not for anything have missed the stay in Horserød, which in my case lasted only two days, from Tuesday to Thursday, 7 October. Naturally it was very sad to watch the arrival of one group of captured refugees after another, poor creatures, most of them penniless, caught during badly organized attempts to escape from the harbors of Dragør, Kastrup, Gilleleje, and many other places. From the famous loft in Gilleleje Church came a long troup of sixty extremely exhausted people, who had undergone a veritable siege by the Gestapo after their hiding place had been betrayed. The German officers stood around having a grand time, laughing at the sight of these worn-out people carrying their luggage and bundles and trying as best they could to protect and comfort the children. Most of them, as well as the other arriving prisoners, had suffered from cold and hunger in their hiding places and their nerves were near the breaking point. But it was surprising to see how quickly they relaxed as soon as they sensed that they weren't to suffer any immediate harm. The tension was over, the game was up, this round was lost. And now they carried on, indomitable, trying to make the best out of things.

The young men and women threw themselves into the work with an almost ferocious enthusiasm, washing and scrubbing, and before long the barracks were shining with cleanliness. The wooden huts were well heated, and both hot and cold water as well as bath facilities were available. The food, eaten in separate barracks entered in strict formation, was plentiful and good, though consisting perhaps of too much rabbit. The prisoners were not subjected to any undue force, malice, or brutality as we had been in Vestre Prison. The tone used by the superior officials was civil, almost polite. The German commanding officer, Captain Jäger, immediately nominated a very well-suited person as spokesman for the prisoners. This was a former circus acrobat who had traveled widely in Germany and therefore was fluent in the language. He carried out his functions with a combination of good sense, zeal, natural authority, and fairness. To serve as his assistant, he named a former cabaret singer who was cheerful and filled with good humor.

GLIMPSES FROM HORSERØD

The readers should know that when I refer to Horserød, in this account, I am referring specifically to a Jewish camp, set up in great haste as a result of the capture of the Danish Jews. The camp was dismantled a few days later when, in heartrending scenes, the Jews were taken to Elsinore and put onto cattle cars bound for Germany. Quite separate from this camp was another in Horserød, that of the "intellectuals" with its roots in the events of 29 August. This camp, too, was in the process of being dismantled. This latter camp also held the Danish Communists, the majority of whom had already been sent to death camps in Germany unless they had managed to escape during the mass flight on 29 August.

The "clientele" of the Jewish camp consisted mainly of stateless emigrants, German and Polish Jews who had come to Denmark during the impending storm in Germany to seek shelter in the streets of Copenhagen. These people were destitute, often not able to speak Danish at all or at best speaking it very brokenly, communicating mostly in German or Yiddish among themselves. In appearance some seemed to be cut straight out of Franzos's tales from Barnov and other towns of The Steppes. They were people the likes of which had never been seen on the streets of Copenha-

Horserød camp, located about nine kilometers west of Elsinore, was well guarded. Electrified wire fence, dogs, and watchtowers with search lights prevented escape attempts. Prior to 29 August 1943 the camp housed several hundred Danish communists whose imprisonment, albeit reluctantly agreed to by the Danish government, was a troubling omen for the Jews. After 29 August 1943, the Germans used the camp for the temporary internment of prominent Danish hostages, and later as the collection point for all the captured Jews.

gen, strange types, stranded on the Danish shores on account of the volcanic eruptions of the Hitler era.

But the camp also housed several people with whom I felt in closer rapport and to whom my thoughts later went out in trepidation and compassion. First of all, Hanna Adler, the aunt of the Bohr brothers [Nobel laureate physicist Niels Bohr and his brother Harold Bohr, professor of mathematics who were part Jewish], had been captured in Dragør with her niece in an abortive attempt to escape. She who was now moving about in the camp with as much serene and aristocratic dignity as back in her school yard. "So now I have experienced being in prison," was the eighty-four-year-old lady's only comment, "*That,* I should never have imagined!" Her only concern was that her friend of many years, the mathematician Dr. Thyra Eibe, would be worried about her, and she asked me to telephone Dr. Eibe the moment I was released to calm her fears.[2]

Then there was Mrs. Asta Krohn, daughter of the honorable Philip W. Heyman who was the founder of the Tuborg Brewery, and widow of Mario Krohn, director of the Danish National Gallery. I also made the acquaintance of a Mr. Philipsen, a merchant and the brother of the deceased painter Sally Philipsen. He and his wife had attempted to escape on a boat but had been shot at from the coast, whereupon the skipper had jumped overboard, leaving the vessel in the care of the drunken helmsman, who had reversed the ship's course back to the shore with such a force that Mrs. Philipsen had fallen into the sea. She was drenched to the bone, but having no change of clothes, had to let the wet ones dry on her body. The fate of one person was especially moving, that of the high-court barrister Moritz Oppenhejm. With his wife, son, and daughter he had boarded a boat that sprang a leak and, though they had been sighted by a passing Danish ship, the captain of that ship had callously refused to take them to the nearby island of Hveen or to any other Danish harbor for that matter. Instead he had signaled the Germans at Kronborg Fort in Elsinore to come and pick up the refugees. Before Hitler's takeover, Moritz Oppenhejm's law firm, perhaps for as many as fifty years, had acted as legal advisors and counsel to Germany and her embassy in Denmark. It was a grim twist of irony that he and his family, of all people, should fall victim to German persecution. The whole family was deported to Theresienstadt where they were confined until their exchange release to Sweden near the end of the war.

Oppenhejm was an admirable character. He and his warm-hearted and energetic wife, being full Jews, had not the slightest chance of being set free, but all the more did he go to the defense of those for whom the tiniest speck of mixed blood might lead to freedom. A born lawyer, he encouraged and consoled his clients, looked carefully into each case, supported them in submitting applications for release by way of the camp's commandant, informed them of what would be important evidence and what they should write, and, if need be, wrote the applications himself. Lighting up one of my excellent *Caminante* cigars, sent to me through Professor Warburg from the 29 August camp, he seemed entirely at ease, at his best when called upon to help his fellow human beings without ever thinking of himself and his own bleak prospects.

Mrs. Arnskov was there, too, the widow of the well-known Judge Arnskov. She was there as a result of her desire to help refugees escape and had been caught along with a large group of them. There were not many other well-known names in the camp, though there were a good many fine elderly spinsters who hadn't managed to get away in time and were now paying the hard price for not having married an Aryan in their youth.

PROFESSOR WARBURG, THE CAMP'S GOOD SAMARITAN

Next to Mr. Oppenhejm, Professor Erik Warburg, the physician [Professor Warburg was the king's physician], came to embody support and help for this colorful group of two to three hundred needy people. He was himself still being detained as prisoner in the adjoining Camp of 29 August and performed the work of ten, thanks to his magnificent physique and his indomitable spirit. In his own camp he had earned not only the affection of his fellow Danes but also the respect of the Germans. The soldiers stood at attention as he gave his medical orders, and, when he walked with the camp commandant, it was *he* who seemed to be in command. Twice a day, in the morning and in the afternoon, he came to the Jewish camp, held consulting hours and dispensed medicine, especially sedatives. The patients formed long queues, for his arrival was eagerly anticipated each visit. The rumors on Thursday that he had been granted a release and would leave the same day was met with widespread sadness. That afternoon he came for his last visit and brought with him a large suitcase filled with apples, sweets, jam, cigars, and cigarettes—leftovers from the abundance of the "intellectuals" in the adjoining camp which he left in my charge to distribute in our camp. A bright light was snuffed out when he left the camp.

THE MASS RELEASE FROM THE CAMP

That very same Thursday, I, too, got out. The camp had become so crowded with incoming prison transports that room was getting scarce. A commission sent over from Dagmarhus was, therefore, assembled to sort out those who were exempt from detention according to regulations and who consequently were to be set free—the half and quarter-Jews as well as the full Jews who were married to Aryans. The result of the day's work was the release of some thirty to forty persons, I among them as the last. Oppenhejm had tirelessly reminded the camp authorities to be sure not to forget the old "editor." When at last I was interrogated, every one of the commission's exhausted members had risen and left the room to stretch his legs, leaving it to the clerk to hold a kind of perfunctory hearing, my case having apparently already been decided. In any case, the clerk, a vile Danish Nazi with heavily padded shoulders, saw his big chance. First he advanced various views against my paper, *Politiken,* then he proceeded with a close investigation of my family lineage, including dates, and birthdays of children and grandchildren. All this, of course, was pointless, as, for example, when I confirmed what he already knew, that my wife was the daughter of A. D. Jørgensen, he asked whether I could produce her christening certificate as proof of her being a genuine Aryan. When I replied, "Is that really necessary?" he angrily flared back, "You are not the one asking questions, it is I, and you are to answer them!" This made for quite an amusing scene. Well, actually this fellow was not altogether harmless. I was told that he used to walk around during breaks in the proceedings depriving the prisoners of the king's anniversary pins which were in their lapels as a symbolic amulet. Based on the description I was able to provide and on additional information about him, I trust he received his just deserts after the war.

In two large trucks, identical to the ones we arrived in, we were driven back to Dagmarhus and then dismissed. The only ones who had to remain in Dagmarhus were the four Aryans who had assisted Jews in their attempts to escape. Among these was a well-known football player and sports coach, who told me during the drive that he had been in the loft in Gilleleje Church and had led the resistance against the German Gestapo when it had besieged the church. He had locked the church despite the Germans' threat to shell it. He had not so much aimed at saving the sixty to seventy people who were barricaded inside and could not be saved as at diverting the enemy's attention from the coast where at that very moment boat after boat was taking off, fully loaded with refugees. If this story, which I have not been able to verify, is true, this sportsman must be deemed an excellent strategist. He had been forced finally to give himself up and had been taken to Horserød. I don't know what happened to him and the others who were kept at Dagmarhus. They were probably delivered to the Danish police and then released.

THE LETTER FROM DR. BEST

Coming out of Dagmarhus overjoyed at my freedom, I crossed the street to my newspaper *Politiken*'s building, and by phone quickly learned that my wife and eldest son had reached Sweden in reasonably good condition, my wife having fallen in the water and hurt her knee badly upon descending from the gangway into the boat in pitch darkness. My other son, I now learned, was still fleeing with his wife and small daughter by way of a route that was considered safer, passing by the islands of Lolland and Falster. My eighty-two-year-old sister had reached Sweden from the peninsula of Stevns. For my part I decided to relax a bit and get my bearings. After talking things over with an old friend in whose hospitable home I stayed, I decided to try to cross the sound in the normal way, with a valid passport. I wanted to leave, that's for sure, as I didn't know how long my Aryan marriage would protect me. There was every reason to fear that new regulations would widen the criteria for the German roundup. In addition to my marriage certificate, dated 1902, I even carried in my notebook a certified copy of the letter from Dr. Best to Svenningsen [administrative head of the Danish foreign ministry] wherein the former confirmed the limits of the roundup. But would these documents save me from further unpleasantness if things came to a pass and I was recognized by Danish Nazis, the more than willing henchmen of the Germans? I was as uncertain of this as I was that a mistake would not be made. And if I first were transported to Theresienstadt, what good would my marriage certificate and Dr. Best's letter do me? And further, the letter didn't even contain any promises of a definitive nature, and even if it had, what then? One more broken promise would be of no importance to the Germans.

Now it developed, strangely, that for a period of a few days

Jews were allowed to obtain passports, valid for "emigration to Sweden," but with the implied proviso that they were never allowed to return to Denmark. But this proviso didn't really matter, for the moment the Germans left the country, it would of course become void. Jewish citizens formed a long queue in front of a temporary passport office next to Langebro in Copenhagen, a little apprehensive lest it be a trap, with the Gestapo lying in wait. It turned out to be on the level. It is my impression that quite a few people obtained passports in this way. I was one of the last lucky ones along with the owner of the well-known stockbrokerage firm of R. Henriques and Son, Carl Otto Henriques. But after the sabotage explosion of "La Tosca," a restaurant frequented by Germans, the Germans ceased immediately the issuance of passports, as a form of revenge. But I had already secured mine.

MY SECOND ATTEMPT TO ESCAPE TO SWEDEN

But before this, I had attempted another escape, once more without success. It was a most valuable experience nevertheless as it provided me with an insight into the large, widespread and carefully organized work devoted to saving Danish Jews from extinction, selflessly carried out at a great personal risk to the people involved. Young people from all walks of life dedicated themselves, their time, strength, and good night's sleep, often their life and health, to this work. Great sums of money, needed for the often expensive transports by car over long distances, poured in from all sides. In the lead were doctors and nurses from the hospitals, ably aided by groups of students.

I was told by an eminent doctor from Aarhus, whose Jewish origin had caused him to flee to Stockholm, that a lady, totally unknown to him, had come up to him in the days before he fled when things were looking bad, saying, "You don't know me, but *I* know *you*. My name is so and so, this is my address and here is the key to my house if you ever should need it." Once when I told this little incident to a lady from Copenhagen who similarly had been in danger, she remarked, "Oh, yes. The same happened to me. At one point I had four keys in my pocket for houses entirely unknown to me."

One day a young man, a stranger to me, was standing in my home, presenting himself to me under an alias. He told me he was a messenger of a well-known person—he gave the name—who had been upset to hear that I was still in town. I had to leave at once. The car was waiting for me and I was given fifteen minutes to pack. I hurriedly pulled together some toilet articles and bundled them in my wife's bag, an old hand at the job now. The whole thing seemed very simple: I would be taken to a hospital, and from there go in an ambulance to somewhere on the coast where a ship would be awaiting me. Things didn't turn out to be that simple after all. Once on the hospital grounds, the ambulance I was in was exchanged for another type of car, in which I continued on in the company of a small working-class family. The husband, a house painter, had married a Jewess and was now escaping with her and their small baby. We were each given a substantial box lunch by the ever-considerate nurses who waved goodbye to us. We were off, driving along the smaller country roads, avoiding the main roads and the towns where we might be conspicuous. The principle was sound, but we got lost several times and had to go back. The maps were studied during the frequent stops. All this took its toll on our over-wrought nerves, but in the end we reached the big forest where young people were standing at spaced intervals to give us directions. Quite an organization had been mounted down at the beach. Some thirty to forty cars were gradually converging. A host of helpers, male and female, were working incessantly to receive some two-hundred anxious refugees, among these a score of children of all ages who were howling and whimpering, wanting to go home. Shelter for a few, but not all, was in a fisherman's cottage. It was very stuffy and difficult to stand inside, couped up with a small child who kept on in an incessant and monotonous litany, "I want to go home." So most of us remained, dejected, in the yard waiting for the boat.

THE GERMAN PATROL BOAT

Yes, the ship, the ship! It still had not arrived. For hours on end our impatient inquiries were met with comforting assurances that it would soon be there. The ship had been sighted, it was approaching, but for some reason or another it didn't dare run into low water where small boats were kept ready to take us out to her. The reason for the delay we didn't learn until the next day. A suspicious vessel had unexpectedly turned up, quite contrary to plan—a German patrol boat. We had no idea why it was anchored at that particular spot; probably it had only run into the creek to escape the gale. If it had had the slightest suspicion of illegal activities going on on the beach, all it had to do was to direct its searchlights onto the shore to confirm its suspicions. But all that happened on board was that a few rockets were sent up, no doubt only for the purpose of orientation. But it was sufficient to create panic on the beach. Our large group immediately performed a somewhat disorganized scramble for the woods, preceded by cars which drove ahead at a leisurely speed to induce some manner of order, finally to vanish for shelter among the trees. We sat in the cars, waiting and half asleep. Not until 4:00 a.m. after many exhausting hours, did we get into a bed, some of us in the nearby manor house of Gjorslev where the hospitable owner, Tesdorpf, and his wife were still up, trying their best, and more, to look after the comfort of their guests.

The next day, the uncertainty repeated itself. The patrol had vanished and we were assured that a ship was now on its way to pick us up, only to be told in the afternoon that the plan had been altered and we were to be driven all the way to the south coast to the island of Falster and ferried to Sweden from there. So having lived through a harrowing day and night, we were now faced with a grim drive of four to five hours, followed, if all went well, by a sea voyage of a minimum of twelve hours in a small boat in storm and hail. This proved too much for an elderly gentleman—so I decided to go back. I had a lovely stay at Gjorslev. The gardens were delightful, even in October, and we were served a delicious lunch. With utmost gratitude I parted from our hospitable hosts and took my seat in one of the many cars returning to Copenhagen. I suppose that in the end the voyage was successful; otherwise we would have heard. The ones who had remained were well looked after while waiting for a second attempt at escape. Warm shelter for the night was procured and the following day food was brought to them by cars, probably prepared and sent by the kitchens of Bispebjerg Hospital.[3]

TAKING THE FERRY TO MALMÖ

For my part, I went on negotiating for a passport, and, four days later, on Saturday, 16 October, I held the precious document in my hand. I saw to it that my furniture was put into storage, took my time packing a couple of suitcases, and on Sunday boarded the ferry for Sweden in the loveliest possible October sunshine, without the slightest problem or hindrance placed in my way, in fact, it was no different from peace time. And yet, not quite. As I embarked, the Danish authorities took from me the remainder of the six thousand kroner, money which ironically I had managed to hold on to while in the German prison and detention camp. When I arrived in Sweden, I was a regular tramp, with only one hundred kroner in my pocket. The ticket to Malmö cost a few kroner, but my two previous attempts at escape had been rather expensive, totaling twenty thousand kroner.

I have often thought that this sum of money, which eventually took me to Sweden, in peace time could have taken me around the world on a luxury liner. I could have enjoyed all kinds of comforts, flirted with beautiful and glamorous "dollar princesses," played badminton in the mornings and danced the night away in the warm luxurious lounge. To have missed such joys! And yet what I in actuality experienced was far more valuable. I saw goodness of heart, I met selfless and unexpected helpfulness, which though I found it surprising at first left me with a deep and everlasting joy that still gives me a warm glow whenever my thoughts return to those days in October 1943.

NOTES

1. Klampenborg and Humlebæk are small seaside villages. The former is only ten kilometers north of Copenhagen and easily reached by a twenty-minute train ride from the city. The latter is another twenty-five kilometers north, some ten kilometers shy of Elsinore.

2. A petition signed by more than four hundred of Mrs. Adler's former students as well as by the mayor of Copenhagen, officials of the Ministry of Education, and others was effective in securing Mrs. Adler's release. She was provided with a special permit to remain in Denmark for the remainder of the war. See Leni Yahill. *The Rescue of Danish Jewry*. Philadelphia: Jewish Publication Society, 1969, p. 490.

3. One of the most active hospitals in helping Jews to escape.

Sam Besekow, the well-known Danish theater personality and author. His recollections of his arrest and escape are bittersweet.

6.

Sam Besekow

Not unlike moths, memories crowd in on me tonight. The swarm is dense, but the memories come as a relief.

I am driving through Gränna, a once important but now insignificant town in Småland, a region of great scenic beauty in Sweden. How often during the "evil years" of my exile in Sweden did I sleep in the local hotel in this Lilliputian town on my way from refugee camp to refugee camp to entertain my compatriots with readings of Hans Christian Andersen or to entertain those of the elderly still in command of their *Mameloschen,* Yiddish, the works of Scholem Aleichem.

Oh, yes! There it is, the home of the childrens' favorite gaily striped pink-and-white candy, the "Polkagrisar," on sale on every street corner and sweet shop in Sweden, its colors competing with the hues of sunsets and the waters of Lake Vättern. And there on icy winter days I met an eagle, perched on a garden wall in the middle of the town, searching for food, its predatory bird's eye resting on my car as it passed to Stockholm.

The memories swarm around my ears . . . Stockholm! And the old city, *Gamla Sta'n!*[1] Those who have never inhaled the fragrance of the Christmas market in *Gamla Sta'n* have never really felt Christmassy. Oh, will I ever forget the small gingerbread figures, dangling in the evening breeze on suspended strings in the

Translated by Ida Pagh (with the assistance of Leo Goldberger). Editor's interpretations appear in brackets and Notes.

market stalls? And the mulled wine and flickering acetylene lamps and the squeak of winter boots and galoshes on the crisp snow? To me, Christmas is forever linked with the years in exile, with the Swedish countryside and people . . . Rowing across Lake Siljan to midnight mass in the glow of flares with my mind weighed down as if by a black rock, dwelling on those left behind on the other side of the sound . . . it felt wonderfully strange and painful, alien and yet familiar . . .

Oh, yes! That was a long time ago . . . or was it? . . . No, it was yesterday. But of course, those who came after this "long time ago" tend to view it all, the war and the Resistance and the Gestapo, as so many bedtime stories and fairy tales and those of us who were involved as wonderland characters.

But let's start at the beginning, going way back . . . In a small theatre in Frederiksberg, an almost rural part of Copenhagen, André Abey's *Noah* was playing, with me in the title role. Not only did we have a voluminous Ark and many animals, but also a Mrs. Noah, a veritable *Hausmutter* [housemother] and matron. The part was interpreted by a Mrs. Emma Rosenstand, who fitted it admirably, for she *was* that kind of *Hausmütterchen,* German-born and married to a Dane, speaking a delightful broken German-Danish. But the moment her German compatriots were standing uninvited in Denmark, there was nothing broken about *her,* and she demonstrated a heart more Danish than most Danes, as did others, such as my former class teacher from school. His face bore the scars of the German dueling tradition and everyone in class had taken it for granted that he was a Nazi sympathizer. But he went underground, machine gun in hand, to join one of the resistance groups.

Turning the page, you find me secretly installed in the hidden attic in Mrs. Rosenstand's villa in the suburbs, out of sight in the manner of Anne Frank in Amsterdam. Loyalty and friendship are like bread and salt and came from many sides. In fact, thousands of others in Denmark acted the same way. And although one is proud that this was so—even a bit surprised today—we know that it was true also in Germany itself, not to mention Holland, only there was no neighboring Sweden offering refuge in those countries. But this overture is preceded by yet a prologue—as is everything else. And we must take a giant's leap backwards, all the way to 1933. Hitler is the victor of the day and has moved into the Chancellery. On the very same day the news hit the front pages, my world-wise father came to me with a new gold cigarette case in hand. As a former refugee from Czarist Russia, he knew what might lie in store for us. "If ever we must flee again," he said, "take this and sell it somewhere so as to get a start!"

From that day on, we waited every day for the inevitable—first the outbreak of the War in 1939, then the German occupation of Denmark on 9 April 1940. And a strange calm fell upon us, for now things could only turn worse . . . some other day . . . some other year . . . Finally the fatal day *did* come, and it is now immediately remembered: 29 August 1943!

Six o'clock in the morning, the doorbell was ringing like mad. We lived on the fifth floor. The bell went on ringing, more and more fiercely. My wife rushed to answer it, uniformed men were standing with machine guns pointing at us, ordering me to come along. Slowly I got dressed as the *Oberführer* walked into our apartment keeping an eye that everything was done correctly. He told my wife, "You'd better make him some sandwiches," at which she heaved a silent sigh of relief. "At least they aren't going to shoot Sam straight away," she thought. From friends in Norway we had heard of the theater director Gleidisch's having been fetched in the same manner to be found shot through the head the next morning. The *Oberführer* watched my wife as she made the sandwiches. Pointing his finger impatiently at the sandwiches, he remarked, "Is that the best you can give him?"

As I walked downstairs surrounded by the men with machine guns, I could hardly keep from laughing. I saw myself as a rather Chaplinesque figure in a tragi-comic farce—the sight we presented must have been ludicrous.

From there on to the mattress-spread gymnasium of Alsgade School, which had been chosen to receive the hundred or so hostages who were taken that day to save the Germans from the disturbances which were impending in Copenhagen as well as in other Danish cities. "*Die hundert besten Köpfe Dänemarks*" ["the hundred best Danish minds"] were in captivity, they boasted. These one hundred heads were to fall, one by one, if . . . well, if the Danish population didn't listen to reason . . .

Green police vans arrived at the school, one after the other, laden with . . . "No, you too! . . . and you! . . . and you! . . . Good morning . . . yes, what a morning." We were all there, scientists, artists, teachers, doctors, and politicians as well as the editors of the major newspapers . . . "Look, the aristocratic actor Henrik Bentzon and the famous actress Else Skouboe! In fact, the Gestapo hadn't wanted him at all, but, to quote him, he had declared: "I shall escort my lady to the scaffold!" The clerk looked at him in astonishment as he couldn't find his name on his lists: "Who are you? Bentzon, you say?" "*Mr.* Bentzon to you, if you please!"

The man in uniform stared at him as did the other Swastica-adorned officer. "Are you Jewish?"

Bentzon threw him a disdainful glance, "Aristocratic looks are not a Jewish prerogative!"

And soon the animals to be slaughtered were herded together in the school's two gymnasiums. The air was thick with talking and questioning—and the "latrine sergeant" was hard at work. No one was allowed to go to the lavatory unless guarded by two men who stationed themselves in front of the open door. And our stomachs were somewhat unsettled as the nervous strain hit our peristaltic movements. Yet somehow we felt a sort of happiness as we gradually discovered how many there were, sharing the same fate. No one knew, of course, what was going to happen to us, and if we were scared this was not without cause, as most of us had a thing or two to hide. I, for one, immediately after 9 April 1940, realizing that no immediate danger was threatening, had started my own private resistance movement.

I had traveled up and down the country, from platform to platform in community halls, folk high schools, everywhere, singing and giving readings of Tucholsky and others.[2] This was a direct sequel to my sojourn in Berlin with the dramaturgist Piscator[3] where the other actors and I were sent out in groups to perform sketches and songs, not scorning the humblest bar in the working-class district of Moabit in our attempt to influence the political scene. Here and there the Brownshirts had gotten there first and we were met with violence, but we believed in the justice of our cause. And yet the Führer clung to his throne despite our efforts, and I pursued my literary crusade, now in the kingdom of Denmark.

In only one place was the show a disaster, in Aabenraa,[4] close to the German frontier (or Apenrade in the jargon of the many local Nazi sympathizers). I wasn't allowed many minutes on the stage before I was thrown out. But as yet it was not customary to kick the fallen in the head, in Denmark, that is. My itinerary also took me to the folk high school of Krogerup. There the then-principal, Professor Hal Koch,[5] and his wife, Bodil (who was later to become minister of cultural affairs *and* to astonish American Secretary of State John Foster Dulles by smoking her mannish cigars!), attended my performance and presented me with a privately printed edition of John Steinbeck's, *The Moon Is Down.*

This book was to become my beacon just as the Kochs became devoted friends, who brightened my life. From the very first, they were wonderful and an inspiration to me; their memory strikes a quiet note in me.

I was struck by the unforgettable serenity of these readings—the more so as the subsequent discussions were heated, although quietly so, as whisperings went on about sabotage and forced labor in Germany. And what was to be done? I was only hurt this once—in Aabenraa—and never again till 29 August, when the interrogation fully demonstrated that the Gestapo was perfectly aware of my previous activities.

Forty years have passed, are gone, and once in a while I have cause to bike through Horserød Plantation[6] in the somber melancholy August nights. The early autumnal twilight throws shadows back to the days and weeks we spent as prisoners here. In 1943. Sadness invades me as I glimpse the barracks half-hidden in the woods—today they serve as an open prison. The chirrupings of the titmice and the hoarse call of a far off pheasant echo the shouts of "toe the line" in those days.

We were not adept at toeing the line—one step out of line and the whole alignment broke down to the eternal despair of the fat little commanding officer. "Gentlemen, gentlemen—you *must* behave. Don't force me to take stricter measures!" Apart from this, he had a habit of stripping half-naked to play football with his cronies outside the barbed-wire fence. He sunned himself before our gaze jumping sloppily around with his tight ball of a belly and obviously enjoying displaying to us what he seemed to think was his perfectly virile and genuinely Aryan beauty.

We spent our time behind the barbwire talking; attending services, readings, and tutorials; and playing games of cards. Outside the fence, Denmark eagerly shared in our fates. We were sent the most incredible things. For instance, the publishing houses sent books en masse and I became responsible for establishing a library. The tobacco factories were no less eager, and when liquor was forbidden it was provided by wine merchants and distilleries, smuggled into camp, camouflaged as scent and hair tonic in the appropriate bottles. The Germans used to wonder at the amount of hair tonic consumed by the Danes.

I still have in my possession a framed handkerchief on which are written in pen and ink the names of 103 people, one big family . . .

The days that led to 29 August had been more or less unpleasant, without my knowing exactly why, they were fraught with nightmares, such as one I had where I saw my mother and father running distractedly around, the sounds of the street were ringing with the infernal din of armoured cars—or screams. Bad dreams of the most cosmic nature were as familiar. One dream in particular remains clear to me to this very day—first a cloud of aircraft grows to an unbearable size and din. My wife and I rush to the window to watch . . . and what we see is a whole formation of great flying animals. In front flies a giraffe, the long neck stretched in front, next come rhinoceroses, buffalos, and a Siberian tiger, all with their legs tucked under them in the manner of flying birds. And then something happens, a hand appears from behind each animal, grabbing and undoing a zipper under the belly. And in the same instant, parachute troops start pouring out and dropping down. Oh, I say to myself, camouflage! Serious-looking men are harnessed in the parachutes, full military equipment in their arms. Slowly, infinitely slowly, they descend past our window. At last a heavily bearded face passes and I cry to my wife, "Wave to him, wave, it's the Russians who're coming!"

The air having been vibrant with rumors, we expected anything. Whisperings were of strict measures being taken by the Germans, as they had already done in Norway—"At last," was the opinion of some, while others mumbled, "Saints preserve us!" No one believed this last rumor—after all, we had managed so far. My wife, however, was busy during those days destroying what she feared might be compromising material . . . and now, here they were, the machine-gun carriers, this early morning at our address, 11 Hollændervej.

In the police van, the first surprises awaited me: "No, you here? . . . Have they taken you too? And you? How about you, I thought you were going to Sweden?" We were silenced by the shout, "*Mund halten!*" ["Shut up!"].

Held in Alsgade School, we fooled around like irresponsible schoolboys, but an ominous silence fell as we were once more shepherded into the vans. We had no idea of our destination. To Vestre Prison? Can't be, we're not going that way . . . The harbor? We knew that ships were lying waiting for human cargo to Germany . . . Suddenly I saw my wife standing on a corner where the van had to make a halt.

She was standing there with one of our friends and from the movements of her lips, I could read what she was spelling, "Horserød Prison Camp!", information which I immediately passed on to the others in the van.

Incidentally, getting to Horserød was not all that simple. The Germans pored over the maps, discussed the route, drove for a bit, went back, turned, gave up, proceeded—we could have done half of the island of Zealand in the time they spent getting there.

The forest . . . the smell of autumnal trees and sandy paths, barbed wire, sun-baked barracks and timid Czech guards who secretly begged for cigarettes, "We're no better off than you!" they whisphered over the fence.

They were *worse* off than we, that we knew, for we inmates had each other. What has not the publisher Bo Bramsen meant to me, this chivalrous polyhistor? What did not Professor Warburg do? . . . he felt at home in the camp, it was not unlike the hospital, he took charge of all and sundry—the Germans too, saving one of them from death. A soldier had been polishing his rifle and had accidentally pulled the trigger, not hurting himself. But another soldier sitting in the room next door had been hit by the bullet as it pierced the wall—I'm ashamed to admit it, but we had our fun from this event.

With theologians I discussed Old Testament translations, and recent plays with the playwrights Soya and Kjeld Abell . . . and

Hal Koch literally saved me from committing the stupidity of my life. On 1 October, as we were being shooed like a flock of geese from the barracks used for meals, we passed a group of Jewish prisoners being driven from vans by heavily armed guards, who prodded the old people with their rifle butts. Panic showed in the prisoners' eyes as they watched our march. They obviously knew this was their last stop on the road. My sight faltered and I grew faint and dizzy as if I were suddenly hit by a high fever—I had heard the same morning of the hunt which had set in for the Danish Jews . . . and I suddenly thought I recognized my parents in this tragic group.

I was later to hear what had really happened to my parents, for of course it was a stroke of feverish imagination which had made me see them among the old people. My parents' neighbors had come to their small house the moment they heard of the ongoing raid on the Jews and forbade them under any circumstances to stay in the house—they were to come immediately to the neighbors' to spend the next few nights. When it turned out that the situation was serious, the eager search for transportation to the immunity of Sweden was started. My father, as if struck down, became apathetic and could not even don his own trousers . . . and mother would not hear of leaving the country as long as I was in prison. Nevertheless with the help of some acquaintances a connection was made whereby ten thousand kroner would see them safely to Sweden—the risks run by the fisherman to himself and his boat would have to be paid for. And hence the gold cigarette case came into good use.

Taking along only a little luggage but dressed in several overcoats, my parents set off in a taxi. The driver immediately knew the situation and drove them to the harbor of Dragør where they were to meet with their friend and the fisherman at an appointed place in the south end of the harbor. They waited for several hours but in the end understood that the ten thousand kroner was gone with the wind. They were in luck and were able to return to town without being snatched up by the Germans. Once back, they were taken in hand by some of my actor colleagues who took them to a place in the Nørrebro neighborhood of Copenhagen. They were unable to remain in their own house, adjacent to ours, for the

Germans had been at our own home and were liable to return at any moment. As a funny detail I may mention that my home in Hollændervej had been visited again in search of *me,* despite my being long since behind bars—the second gang apparently was unaware of what the first had been doing.

The activities in Denmark were indeed surprising during those days. The first police van had hardly rolled out before the whole nation became involved in hiding the Jews, spiriting them away, organizing groups to help them get away right under the Germans' noses. Young people from all walks of life offered themselves, risking heavy penalties, even their lives. Great sums poured in, for money was imperative. The general hospitals, doctors, nurses, and medical students were at the head of the action, filling beds with people whose physiognomies gave the lie to the traditional Danish names of "Hansen" and "Petersen" under which they were hospitalized. Eventually they were taken in ambulances and taxis to the rescue boats. On the street corners, milkboys were stationed to whistle into fingers as a signal whether the coast was clear, or not.

The confusion of those first days of course resulted in ridiculous episodes, episodes that call for a smile:

My present wife, Jette, was one of the pioneers in the Danish resistance movement. (Many years later, she was one of the Heroes, the little group of six invited to New York to receive a standing ovation as the representatives of Danish resistance fighters on the occasion of the fortieth anniversary of the liberation from the Germans.)

Jette, today a renowned barrister, reminisces:

> "The destination of our transportation was the village of Rødvig on the peninsula of Stevns, where a fisherman was waiting for us. The taxi hurried along as a German police van going at even greater speed overtook us and, stopping in front of us, forced the taxi to a halt. There we were, three "transporteurs" and six Danish Jews, our hearts in our throats. A Gestapo man flung the door open, threw one glance at us and shouted in a voice of command, "*Sie sind ja Juden!*" [You are Jews!"] "Well, what had you expected!" I retorted. Then the taxi was searched from top to bottom, even the seats were taken out into the road. When the search was

Jette Hecht-Johansen became a member of the Danish resistance while still a student. An attorney by profession, she has devoted a lifetime to civil-liberties causes. She was recently awarded the coveted Ebbe Munck prize for peace by Queen Margrethe II of Denmark. Jette Hecht-Johansen is married to Sam Besekow.

over, the taxi driver was ordered to go about his business while we others were told to board the van to sit on two long benches in the middle with six Gestapo men, carrying machine guns, in front and six behind, the latter also pointing at us with their guns. We were strictly forbidden to talk to each other, but adjusting a shoelace here and searching for a handkerchief there and a thousand other little devices made it possible for us during the long drive to Copenhagen to whisper this and that to each other, and in the end we had made up a story for the benefit of the interrogation by the Gestapo in its headquarters, Dagmarhus, in Copenhagen. We arrived there at midnight and, as expected, were interrogated separately but were able to come up with an identical tale. I was questioned by an exceptionally loathsome Gestapo man who ended by growling at me, "What will your father say to your behavior, you're only a child!?" "He will be awfully angry and please don't tell him if you meet him!" I replied. I'm not sure whether he swallowed this or not, and yet, the Germans were naive and rigid to a degree. During the interrogation I had stuck to the story of the Jews' being only half and quarter Jewish, and as such they were not wanted by the "benignant" Germans. We said that we had been going to a party at my uncle's at Stevns. The Gestapo man couldn't have believed me entirely for he uttered several threats of the "grim" instruments they kept in the basement to make me talk . . . or, as he said, "In Germany we could make good use of young girls for our research!"

I was then locked into a room the size of a broom closet. During the drive from Stevns my friends had managed to pass on to me a wad of notes, in all ten thousand kroner, which had been intended for the fisherman. The idea of giving it to me was that we didn't suppose that a girl would be searched in the middle of the night as there would probably be no women on duty in Dagmarhus at that hour. We proved to be right. I managed to slip this great big wad of money into my brassiere—never before or since have I had as magnificent a bust. Now, were this money to be found, the game would be up so I let them understand that I needed a bathroom very badly. A German soldier took me there, standing in front of the door, the toes of his boots protruding into the cubicle from under the door.

I tried desperately to flush the notes down the toilet, but there were a lot of them, all too many, and I was left with an awful lot—and there was no time to spare. So I rolled them into a tight ball and stuffed the rest into the drain-pipe. Whew! And came giggling back into the guards' room where we then sat the whole night through without food or drink. We chattted with the soldiers on duty who turned out to be as fed up with the war as we were—they were mere draftees who only cherished one dream, to return to their families.

At this point we were having quite a party, and my face was splitting in a large grin when "my" Gestapo man returned to the room. He flew into a formidable rage and ordered me to turn my chair to the wall. "I guess the young Miss would profit more from looking at the painting on the wall!"—a huge reproduction of a Hitler portrait.

At last, in the afternoon, we were told that we were to be moved to Vestre Prison where the Danish police came a little later to pick us up. They saluted the Germans in polite military fashion and ordered us in brusque terms to "Come along!" This we did and were seen by the Germans to the door of the waiting police van. Heels clicked and salutes were made and the Danish officers banged shut the door to the van. The three of us felt that the situation looked hopeless. But looking at the smiling faces of the policemen we heard four short but welcome words, "Hungry, aren't you?" Once arrived in the police station we reenacted the interrogation scene (in a kind of "benefit performance") putting the finishing touches on what we had told the Germans—the statements had to be in perfect mutual conformity—and were then told, "Now we let you out through the back door—and please see to it that you disappear, the sooner the better, to Sweden!"

We all arrived safely in Sweden a couple of days later, including our Jewish friends who were anything but quarter- or half-Jewish—they were all full Jews!

So Jette concludes her story.

My parents had had an almost identical experience—succeeding in the second attempt where they had failed in the first.

I had an old schoolmate from the Johannes School to whom I felt very close, Jørgen Gersfelt. We had been as identical twins during the last three years in school. After leaving school (he with a fine grade A matriculation certificate and I lagging considerably behind) we had packed a tent and sleeping bags onto our bikes and had gone on a tour of Europe to visit the battlefields of the Great War. This was in 1930, so during the trip we also learned a thing or two about the ways of the Brownshirts in Germany. I can't be sure that this was the reason that, the moment he heard of the raids on the Danish Jews, Jørgen immediately set about organizing transports to Sweden. But at any rate he proved to be a superb organizer of transportation from the harbor of Snekkersten (where he was a general practitioner)—he mobilized all available fishing boats and motor launches, even row boats were not spurned. Jørgen discovered the whereabouts of my parents—he was as dear to them as he was to me—picked them up himself and saw them onto the train to Snekkersten. This train was so crammed with Jews that, at a glance, anyone would have guessed what was going on, what with heavy luggage, children crying in the arms of frightened mothers—a Gypsy caravan on rails. During the first few days 1,100 people were saved, then the Gestapo got the idea and arrests and captured ships followed. Jørgen was magnificent, turning his private home into a bedlam of refugees on the run, sleeping everywhere on the floors and in the hallways—and he personally escorted my parents to the coast of Sweden, just as he dispensed sedatives to the children to prevent them from making noises that might arouse the suspicions of the Germans. Jørgen Gersfelt will live forever in my mind, and I pay tribute to his memory.

A rumor reached my parents, once they were safe in Malmö in Sweden, that I had been either hanged or shot . . . so when at last we met in Malmö, it was as if they had seen a ghost. My mother broke completely down in tears and my father almost fainted.

But let's return to Horserød Prison Camp on that day when I suddenly stood eye-to-eye with the large group of old Jewish prisoners. Hal Koch, who was walking beside me, foresaw what was going to happen, that in despair I would throw myself at the Germans. So he grabbed me hard, twisting my arms behind my back, and didn't let go of me till we were safe in our own barracks where he flung me, sobbing my heart out, to my plank bed.

It could be that at that very same instant Mrs. Koch, in tacit understanding with her husband, stepped in front of the supreme German commander in Denmark, Dr. Best, and, as the representative of a nationwide women's protest group, declared: "At first we were wondering at the German's abuse of force, then we hated it—and from now on we shall despise it!" This was what Hal and Bodil were like.

Over my bed in my present home on Ceresvej in Fredriksberg hangs a small watercolor of the barracks where I shed tears over the tragic sight I had seen—in this little sketch the painter and woodcarver Otto Bülow demonstrated the great ease of his art. He presented the sketch to me on the day he was released from Horserød so that I could have a memento of the time we spent together . . . shortly after his release he was shot dead by a gang of

The outspoken Bodil Koch, wife of Hal Koch, became Denmark's minister of culture. She is seen here, cigar in hand, with American Secretary of State John Foster Dulles in 1958.

Danish Nazis, "Hipo" men.[7] Horserød Prison Camp has subsequently proved a traumatic experience to us all, a mythlike legacy from which we can't liberate ourselves.

What happened then in the camp of the intellectuals? Well, the sheep were separated from the goats—those of the Jews who were married to Aryans were allowed to withdraw to their sleeping quarters while those of the Jews who had Jewish spouses were gathered together and transported to the harbor to be put on board and taken to Theresienstadt, the concentration camp from which not all were to return. And gradually, as the tension was relieved in Copenhagen, we were pushed back into life. This is where Mrs. Rosenstand took care of me, installing me in the attic of her Klampenborg villa.

At first I walked about freely, not giving flight a thought. Then one day I met Kjeld Abell:

"Aren't you in Sweden?", he asked.

"Why should I be?"

"You're crazy. Things are getting hot; you'd better get out!"

"No one will hurt me; I'm married to an Aryan!"

"How long do you think that will protect you? Whatever Dr. Best may say, the word of a German is not to be relied upon. We can't have you walking around in Copenhagen looking the way you do!" (He himself had had his hair dyed).

"Now, come on, Professor Warburg wouldn't think of going!"

"Maybe not, but he's the king's physician; they wouldn't dare to touch *him!*"

"I'm a stage director in the Royal Theatre, won't that help?"

"Don't be silly—we've got to get you out of here!"

He had his way. It was arranged for my wife and me to board a boat in the the harbor of Nyhavn, in the center of Copenhagen. Nothing could be safer, no German in his right mind would believe that anyone would flee from there.

Then I heard of the most recent arrests and I shut up in more ways than one, not leaving my little room. Then word came about the date set for the flight and the road we were to take. On the very same night I was supposed to leave, a strange event took place.

Protected by the blackout and shut hermetically in a closed van, I was ferried from Klampenborg to the film studios in Hellerup in order to play the finishing scenes in a film which would otherwise have had to be scrapped. It was a farce in which I played the role of a foul Chinese gangster who was supposed to be disarmed by the hero—if this hadn't happened, the story would never have ended. Our secret crew included myself, the director Johan Jacobsen, and the photographer. The lights were put on and we filmed the two scenes, but as I was the only cast member present, I had to act as if my adversary were sitting in front of me at the table or in a chair so that the technicians later, on some other day, could combine my scenes with the other half. Having no cues was rather difficult and I had to pretend to be listening and reacting to what was (not) being said on the other side of the table.

Suddenly we heard steps approaching and hurriedly put out the lights. Had we been discovered? Was the Gestapo on our tracks?

The door opened and to our immense relief the film director Tage Nielsen entered.

"Just to tell you that you're leaving in a couple of hours. I have written to Dr. Dymling, head of Swedish Films Inc.—he'll see to you when you're there. And here you are, one hundred dollars, that will take care of you for a start!" The same situation everywhere—helping hands stretched out.

In the dark of night my wife and I squeezed into herring cases, thoughtfully provided with breathing holes. Actually the cases could barely contain a human body and we lay in our boxes cramped like unborn babies. In this way we were hoisted down into the hold, the only refugees on the boat. If my parents had in vain paid the original ten thousand kroner, later to be supplemented by my father's paying for some who were destitute, Henny and I got across without paying at all. At this time the resistance organizations were able to pay for the refugees.

We lay low in the hold, waiting till noon when at last I heard the noise of the engine starting, thump, thump. Then I heard voices—in German—and the sound of booted feet, tramp, tramp. The steps came to a halt right next to our boxes, but as they were tacked down there should have been no cause for alarm. And then we heard the feet leaving the boat once more and the ship left the harbor. On our way we were boarded by a patrol boat, but there was nothing to inspect on our boat.

At last we were in Swedish waters and could break out of our cases into fresh air. Legs, arms, and back had to be straightened out almost by force, to such a degree had they been cramped. A bottle of champagne was opened, "Welcome to Sweden!" These words were to follow us for the rest of our years in exile.

They were not hollow words—everywhere I was met by, "Welcome! What can we do for you? How can we help you? Are you in want of anything?" Apartments were put at my disposal, the theaters opened their gates wide to me, the actors were flocking around me and became more than colleagues, friends for life.

Now don't get the impression that we forgot the great darkness outside our door. When we went to the harbor in Malmö and looked across to Denmark, it hung over the familiar coastline. And took up a good part of our thoughts, hours and days, irrespective of our other activities. Our thoughts went out to home—and to Theresienstadt. We took a deep breath, "I'm ALIVE!—why *me?*" We could't get away from it. And the days, the years went by; I saw my cousins, much my juniors, grow up; some married and had children.

I went on living. I remember the first summer in Stockholm's archipelago . . . The sea, a brilliant sky, warm cliffs and charred fish on a grill, the boat for Waxholm carrying summer guests to the little islands . . . I remember people walking in the streets. Doors opened wide to receive me. If once in a while I suffered the pangs of the dreaded "refugee's trauma" I sent them packing . . . I remember concerts in the concert hall, where I gave readings of the poetry of the Resistance. The reception I got was unforgettable, as were the ovations after the opening nights, in particular the one for the play by Kaj Munk, *Niels Ebbesen,* about Denmark's famous national hero . . . at the time of the first performance, Kaj Munk had been murdered by the Nazis . . . the ovation was not directed at me, nor at the play, but at Denmark. And this is how I remember the last night of them all, the night of 4 May 1945, never to be forgotten. Chance would have it that this was an opening night too.

The Chinese Variety in Stockholm was not a dance show but a vaudeville theater. I had been hired to get the most crazy revue ever seen in Stockholm on its feet. This is meant literally, as the revue was all dance and acrobatics. The success was as crazy as the job, people queued up for days, storming the booking offices. The title given to the play was in keeping with it all, *The Crazier the Better.* The cast was a crazy lot, too, a veritable refugees' show, Norwegians, Danes, Swedes, Czechs, Italians, English, and Dutch—Danish ballet, Swedish comedians, a Norwegian master of ceremonies, Italian acrobats, sketches, lyric songs, magician's acts—everything was crazily combined in one show.

The fourth of May 1945.

The audience crowded the theatre. The house was full. Palpitations of the heart, agitation, the theater was vibrating with a strange murmur, the seats were clattering, suddenly a shrill laughter was heard in one place, in another someone coughed. Hush! . . . Why hush? I found the sound disquieting. "Programs!" The voices of the program vendors sounded strange. "Chocolate! Ice cream!" There was something awfully wrong about it all, as if all the voices were dampened. A strange mood had invaded the audience, and upstage we were all aware of it, and felt it too.

Strange rumors had traveled the streets of Stockholm—Hitler was now reduced to ashes in his impregnable bunker. It was said to be a fact! How long would this remain a fact?

Damn it, this Hell couldn't go on forever. From the fashionable restaurant Bern's Rooms to the humblest of cafes, whispering and gossip had invaded the city . . .

Now! Ought to happen at any moment . . . And yet . . . who would believe it? Hadn't we heard the news too many times already, each time it was as if a flame pierced our hearts—we're going home! That little word, "home," was constantly on our lips. All of us. The refugees. The "immigrants" as we would be called today, we who lived and breathed for this "China Variety" which had taken us to heart, had cuddled us and looked after us so that we could survive, waiting for the moment when we would really be able to go home and not only subsist on a dream that was wearing thin. We knew that reality in the form of armored divisions was coming nearer every minute, but how close was this "nearer?" And constantly our antennae were out, for who would know, and when? . . . Hence we felt this heartrending anxiety, this is why we felt that the orchestra sounded quite different from the night the conductor first struck up the overture. Was it a matter of Hope's no longer being suppressed by vanquishing Reason? No, it couldn't be; there was something in the air; the audience too was somewhat more restless than usual, was listening in another way . . . and the applause that accompanied each number . . . different?

And then it happened. Come on, Sam, give us a sober account and don't let sentimentality run away with you—

To this day I can hear the phone ringing in the office . . . Damn it, if only it won't be heard on the stage and create a distraction. "Yes, who is it, ringing and disturbing us in the middle of the play?" The manager Bengt Sterner steals out from the little door, leading onto the stage, approaches me, whispering that there is a Dane on the phone who insists on speaking to me. "Here? Now? In the middle . . . Let him go to H——, this is too much!" "He *insists,*" Sterner says, "it's a matter of life and death!" I fall silent— There is only one thing in the world which is a matter of life and death and I hurry to take the receiver . . . A voice is whispering, "The Germans have capitulated, Denmark is liberated!" "No!— I've had enough! You've played that hoax on us before, it's no laughing matter. Why do you *do* such things, it's too much!"

In fact, this had happened a few times before, not as a matter of ill but of the best of wills. And every time it had come as a shock that it had taken days to get over. The bearer of the good news had no doubt believed what he was saying. But that made the disillusionment so much more the worse when eventually it came.

The voice on the phone protested, "You must believe me! It's true. This time it's serious. It's unbelievable, but it's true. I'm sending a man over to you to convince you that I'm right!"

The messenger came at lightning speed, sent from the English consulate. The Germans *had* capitulated. Denmark was through with them.

A hush fell backstage. A dumbfounded surprise. A silence which was interruped by broken sobs. And during this hush, the cast was playing on like mad on the stage, the play tumbled on the boards to the infinite delight of the audience.

Soon, I noticed *him,* a man who was half-hidden in the semi-obscurity of the proscenium. I became aware that he was crying, and that he didn't want others to see. He cried, fit to break your heart, couldn't help himself. Then suddenly he turned toward the rest of us who were preparing to enter the illuminated stage, stammering, eyes glistening, "Congratulations, dear friends, damn it, congratulations! Denmark is free—but what about us Norwegians? What about all my friends, my family in Grini, when are they going to be set free?"

He threw out his hands in an impotent gesture, they hung limply in the air. This was our Norwegian master of ceremonies,

Herbert. He had understood the situation perfectly—it could still be a matter of hours, days even, before Norway got rid of "them," and anything could happen in the meantime.

We wanted to comfort him but he stopped us, saying in a voice thick with tears, "You have to tell them, down there in the audience!" No, that's no good, we argued, we're going to spoil their evening for them, they've paid for their tickets and want their money's worth. He insisted, and stepped upon the stage.

"Ladies and Gentlemen—just now we have been informed that the Germans have capitulated in most of . . . Denmark is liberated!"

You might as well have dropped a bomb in the theater. People jumped up from their seats, embracing, rushing the stage and the orchestra, throwing programs into the air. A volcano had erupted. Those who were seated on the balcony didn't even descend the stairs—they jumped right into the stalls, no, they *flew*. It's a wonder that no one was hurt. Strangers embraced and kissed each other, falling into each other's arms. The audience behaved more crazily than the vaudeville company, crying, yelling, weeping, dancing. But as the orchestra started playing the Danish national anthem, "King Christian", all fell instantly silent, struck by emotion. As still as statues they stood, linking hands, and singing for joy—and pain. The audience became one body, one voice, echoing, at least over half of Stockholm, with the Swedish anthem, "*Du gamla, du fria* . . ."

Yes, liberty had returned, the flight was over, sorrow changed to joy. It was over.

Is it over? The war was won—but did we win the peace?

NOTES

1. Gamla Sta'n, which means simply the "Old Town," is the way Swedes often refer to Stockholm in a sentimental vein.

2. Kurt Tucholsky (1890–1935) was a major German satiric writer whose polemics against nationalism, orthodoxy, and militarism forced him into Swedish exile in 1929. His books were burned by the Nazis and this lead to his suicide.

3. Erwin Piscator (1893–1966) was a veteran director in Berlin who, along with Bertolt Brecht invented "epic theater" in the twenties.

4. Aa (or å) in Danish has the vowel sound of *awe,* hence Aabenraa would be pronounced ôbenrô; certainly not Apenrade.

5. Professor Hal Koch (1904–1963), a theologian and church historian, is also mentioned in Jørgen Hæstrup's article (p. 32) for his inspirational lectures on Grundtvig in 1940 and for his leadership role in the Union of Danish Youth. His emphasis was on maintaining a unified national stance, based on democratic ideals, as the bulwark against Nazism. (See illustration p. 178).

6. Horserød Plantation was the site in northern Zealand about nine kilometers west of Elsinore, used as a prison camp by the Germans during the occupation of Denmark.

7. "Hipo" (Hielfs Polizei) refers to the Danish-German auxiliary police force, which numbered some seven hundred Danish traitors. Their task was to terrorize the population, to serve as a threat against the resistance movement.

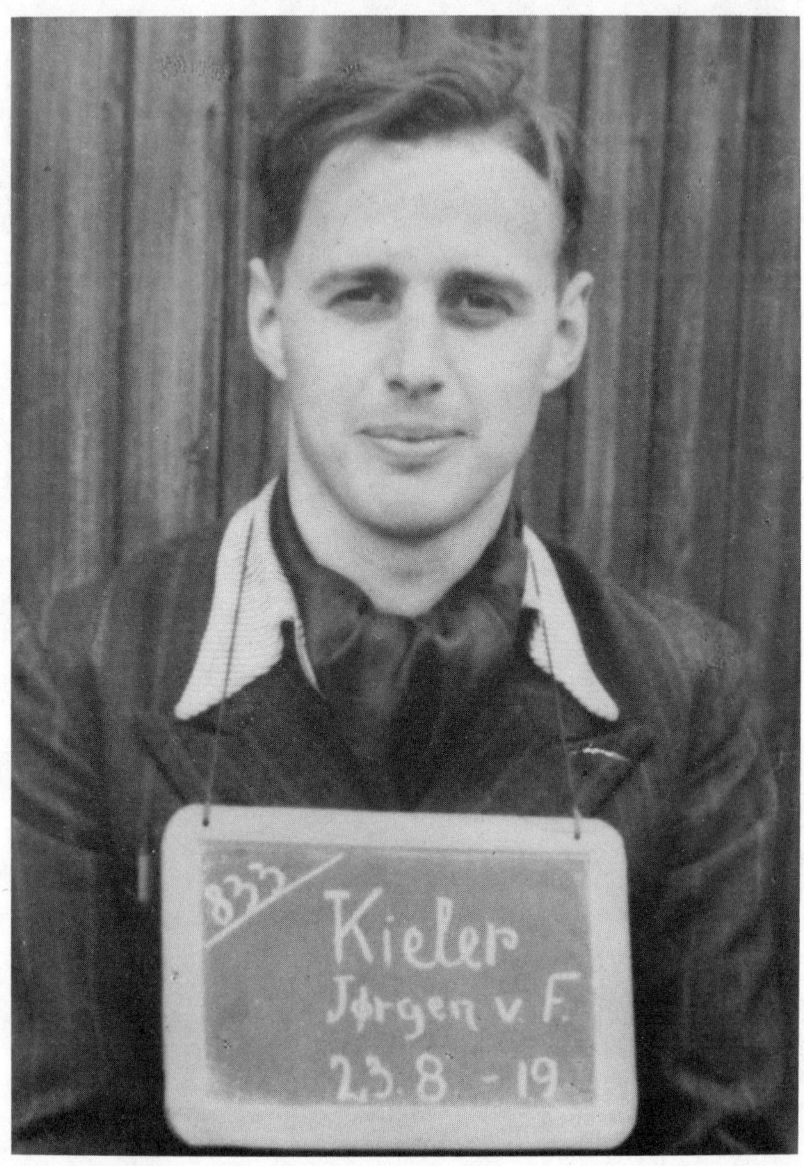

Dr. Jørgen Kieler in his student days worked in the Danish resistance movement, first in connection with the illegal paper *Frit Danmark,* then in organizing escape routes for Jews, and finally as one of the leaders of *Holger Danske,* the sabotage group. He was arrested in February 1944 and deported to a German KZ Camp. He is now a leading researcher at the Danish Cancer Institute.

7.

Jørgen Kieler

Early in the morning of 9 April 1940 I was awakened by the noise of aircraft flying low over Copenhagen. I was sharing a small apartment in the center of the city with my oldest sister, Elsebet. We were both students, coming from Jutland, where our father was a medical practitioner.

Before we started our studies in Copenhagen we had the opportunity to study at universities in Germany, France, and England for one year. I had been a witness to Hitler and Mussolini's meeting in Munich that was followed by the Austrian *Anschluss* and later on the occupation of Sudetenland. I came to Copenhagen in August 1939 a few weeks before Hitler attacked Poland.

We were worried, but our worries were mainly due to the military passivity on the western front after the English-French declaration of war and to the Russian attack on Finland. We did not expect an attack on Denmark. After all, a treaty of nonagression had been signed by the German and Danish governments on 31 May 1939. But the continuous noise from the aircraft over Copenhagen in the early morning of 9 April roused a suspicion that we had been betrayed.

We got dressed and hurried down to the streets where we were stopped by German soldiers. Our suspicion was confirmed: Denmark was no longer a free country.

The German invasion left the Danish people in a paralyzing state of despair, frustration, anger, and shame. These feelings continued for nearly a year, into 1941. One must understand that Denmark was a split country that had not yet recovered from the economic and social problems of the thirties.

In 1941, we Danes experienced reunion of political parties and social groups, all of which gradually realized their common cultural heritage and their common goal: national independence and democracy. Nazi sympathizers remained, but they were a very small and despised minority. The national reunion triggered numerous meetings, during which Danish cultural traditions, literature, and national songs were recognized as a treasure belonging to all Danes.

However, the Danish government and most Danes lived in the delusion that in spite of the occupation Denmark could remain neutral. It was not yet realized that an occupied country has a choice between two alternatives, i.e., collaboration with the enemy or active resistance.

The realization of this fact started to dawn upon us, when Danish Communists, against all laws and without having committed any crime, were arrested by the Danish authorities upon a German demand after the German atack on the Soviet Union on 22 June 1941.

It became even more clear when the Danish government was forced to join the Anti-Comintern Pact in September of the same year.

At this time my younger brother Flemming, and one of my younger sisters, Bente, had joined us. We had moved to a bigger apartment close to the university. Although we came from a conservative family which was extremely upset by the Russian attack on Finland, we felt that the arrest of the Danish Communists was a crime for which we found no excuse. We participated in the large demonstration organized by the students against the Danish acceptance of the Anti-Comintern Pact, and had our first battle with the police.

This was our first attempt to offer active resistance. It was followed by a long period of frustration. I had a feeling that a resistance movement was being born. But how is such a movement organized? What kind of resistance is possible, and how far will it go?

It soon became clear that the Danish people were divided once more, this time between a large majority preferring passive resistance and a small but growing group of men and women who wanted the so-called Norwegian conditions[1] or an active fight against the Germans. The goal was the same for both groups—national independence and democracy—but the means were different. It was not only a question of strategy or courage, but it was also a question of ethics. "What will you do if the Gestapo enters into the room to shoot your younger brother?" was my question to one of my sisters. "Protect him with my body, but I will not carry arms," was the bold answer. In 1942 we were still waiting to see what was going to happen and so the discussion continued. In April 1942 the first illegal newspaper appeared, and during the summer sporadic actions of sabotage occurred. In a radio speech Prime Minister Vilhelm Buhl warned against sabotage and asked the people to inform the police about all persons suspected of sabotage. I saw this as treason.

The growing resistance movement had to face two enemies, the Danish authorities and the Germans. At this time I had finished my preclinical studies at the medical faculty of the University of Copenhagen and I was ready to give up my studies to join the resistance movement. Finally in December 1942 I succeeded in making contact with the other students working for the illegal newspaper, *Frit Danmark* (Free Denmark).

Soon our apartment was turned into a printing office that during the spring of 1943 became the headquarters for a group of students who produced illegal papers and books. The rapidly growing illegal press, which had a strong influence on the population, combined with increasing German pressure, helped to bring about several strikes and actions of sabotage.

On 27 January 1943, the Royal Air Force made an attack on Burmeister and Wain, a big shipbuilding yard in the center of Copenhagen. A number of people were killed but the yard was not hit. This made it clear to me that sabotage might serve three important purposes: political pressure on the collaborating Danish politicians; damage to the industry working for the Germans; and protection of Danish lives that might be lost during air raids.

The discussion between the pacifists and activists continued. In one of the illegal papers published by the students, sabotage carried out by factory workers was characterized as an important

Saboteurs tended to be quite young, often no more than seventeen years of age. The Danish patriots not only engaged in sabotage but operated the illegal press, intelligence, courier and escape services, and an underground army, performing magnificently despite the constant danger of capture. Montgomery called the Danish underground "second to none." The total cost was high, however: more than 6,000 arrested, tortured, and sent to various prisons and concentration camps, with more than 600 dead and many left scarred. To this should be added the loss of 1,450 merchant seamen who in April 1940 chose to head for various Allied ports to join the war against the Axis powers.

contribution to the fight against the Germans, but at the same time the students were warned that they were not qualified to participate in sabotage; their contribution should be the illegal press.

When capital punishment for sabotage was introduced it was obvious to me that such a distinction between workers and students could not be maintained. Life was equally important to both groups. Through a friend in my native town, Horsens, I got my first explosive material, and together we made our first attempt to

Members of the Danish underground are seen here being instructed in the use of British automatic weapons, which were regularly dropped by parachute. In addition to these guns, the Danish resistance movement developed its own homemade arsenal of weapons and ammunition. The resistance movement grew by leaps and bounds following the successful rescue of the Jews.

blow up a railway bridge. We were completely unsuccessful and realized that we needed instruction, weapons, fuses, detonators, and explosives. We decided to continue our efforts, and a division of our group was planned.

On 23 March a general election for parliament was held. It proved the democratic sentiment of the Danish people and the insignificance of the small, despised Nazi party. But it was also the last manifestation of the delusion that an occupied country can remain neutral. Active resistance grew continuously and on 29 August 1943 the government resigned. The chief of the Danish navy, Admiral Vedel, ordered the Danish fleet to be sunk by its crew. The Germans were forced to take over, and from then on, there was only one front.

Danish soldiers were detained in their barracks. A cousin of mine was a naval cadet. He and his colleagues were interned at the naval headquarters in Copenhagen. They started to smuggle machine guns, pistols, and ammunition from the headquarters to our apartment.

The resignation of the Danish government was a victory for the resistance movement, but it did not mean that the Danish people were united, and it is very likely that the discussion concerning active versus passive resistance would have continued if it had not been for two serious German mistakes.

In the middle of September the first execution of a Danish saboteur took place. Nobody could be in doubt any longer that participation in active resistance implied willingness to risk one's own life. Were the supporters of passive resistance willing to make a similar sacrifice?

They got an opportunity to answer that question about two weeks later, when the Germans made their second blunder. They began to persecute Danish Jews. It was the opportunity to "protect one's younger brother with one's own body." The opportunity was seized by numerous people who had been living in an ethical conflict for several months.

Due to the courageous smuggling of weapons from the naval headquarters we were no longer unarmed. Weapons, however, were not enough to save Jews. We needed money and ships to carry the refugees to Sweden. The financial problems were solved within forty-eight hours. Klaus, a young member of our group, was well acquainted with most of the larger estates in the surroundings of Copenhagen. Together with my sister Elsebet, he made a weekend trip to these places, and when they returned, they had one million kroner, a considerable fortune. Additional funds were raised by other members of our group, and many refugees were also able to make significant contributions.

Through their personal contacts, two young girls, Ebba Lund and Henny Sinding, who had joined our group, got in touch with several fishermen and the crew of a small supply ship which made daily tours to a lighthouse in the middle of the sound between Denmark and Sweden. In this way, we established two important escape routes from Copenhagen. Finding Jews, bringing them to the harbor, and organizing and protecting their embarkation became our most important tasks during the following weeks. Ebba and Henny were always there to see them on board. We found ourselves in an emergency situation where risks had to be taken. It was an inspiring experience to witness how the willingness to help fellow citizens in extreme danger united the Danish people. All discussion concerning passive and active resistance stopped, and I am happy to say that during this period we did not meet with any traitors. Occasionally German patrols appeared at the time of embarkation, but they always retired when they discovered that armed saboteurs, Danish policemen, and fishermen were prepared to defend the refugees. About 1,500 persons were rescued via our two routes, without the loss of a single life.

We did, however, lose one of our friends, Cato Bakman. Cato was a medical student who did not want to become a saboteur, but he was not afraid to risk his life in the service of the illegal press and the rescue organizations. One day he was surprised by the Gestapo in an apartment belonging to a surgeon at the Bispebjerg Hospital. He jumped out of the window from the second floor but was hit by German bullets. Severely wounded, he was taken to the emergency room of the hospital, where he died in the arms of the nurse on duty. She was his wife. They had married a few weeks before. She buried her young husband and continued his work.

There are several reasons for the successful rescue of Danish Jews. Most important is, of course, the well-known warning by Georg Duckwitz, the German attaché, who deserves more credit than any one person for alerting us Danes to the impending action against the Jews. Nearby neutral Sweden, separated from Denmark by the narrow waters, was another important factor. The inability of the German navy to supervise the long Danish coastline also played a role, and internal German disagreements were of great help. The rivalry between the German high commissioner, Werner Best, and the head of the German army in Denmark, General von Hanneken, made the persecution inefficient. While these were important factors, the reaction of the Danish people was a decisive factor. In my opinion, the discussion concerning passive versus active resistance represents a background offering a reasonable psychological explanation for this reaction, but a traditional humanistic attitude to life and the absence of serious anti-Semitism in Denmark played their part too.

Many of us came from the organized resistance, but others came spontaneously when they were needed. National independence and democracy were our common goals, but the persecution of Jews added a new and overwhelming dimension to the fight against Hitler: human rights. Our responsibility toward and our respect for the individual human being became the primary goals of the struggle, a struggle which required a maximum of moral and physical strength from the rescuer and the rescued alike, and above all from those who were caught by the Germans.

When the stream of refugees ceased, our group continued the sabotage without further ethical discussions. A number of cadets, who had been released from internment, joined the students. Furthermore, contact was established with the remaining two members of a sabotage organization called *Holger Danske* (Holger the Dane). The other members of the organization had escaped to Sweden after several successful actions against places of German interest, including Forum, a big exhibition hall which they were going to use for the accommodation of German troops. The Holger Danske organization was named after a legendary giant who is expected to wake up from his sleep in the cellar of Kronborg castle and defend Denmark when our country is in danger.

The two remaining Holger Danske saboteurs, called Finn (Jens Lillelund) and John (Svend Otto Nielsen) had contact with the British Special Operation Executive (S.O.E.) which organized resistance in the occupied countries. John became the leader of our group which was called Holger Danske 2 (HD2). He was an experienced saboteur. Later I learned that he was a teacher of mathematics before he joined the resistance movement. Now we had weapons and instruction. Explosives we obtained from a limestone quarry (by bribery using some of the money left after the rescue of the refugees), a German railway wagon, and from the S.O.E.

HD2 became one of the most active groups during the following four months. It carried out a total of twenty-five actions against factories which produced radio equipment, sights for bombers, uniforms, and other war material. Our greatest achievement was the action against the B&W shipbuilding yard in Copenhagen, which the Royal Air Force had missed in its air raids in January 1943, and a big steel mill in Jutland. Our targets also included factories producing dried milk and canned meat for the Germans.

One of numerous acts of sabotage against the railways aimed at paralyzing the movement of German troops, ammunition, and hired labor. This form of sabotage (reaching a total of 2,156 acts whereby 8,000 stretches of rail and 25 bridges were detroyed) was to engage some 15,000 men and women in the resistance movement at various times. Sabotage activities became increasingly sophisticated and from 1942 on were directed via Anglo-Danish channels. With the help of the underground, the RAF targeted sites for strategic bombing, keeping Danes running in and out of shelters.

Even the much-beloved Tivoli, the famous Danish amusement park in the center of Copenhagen, became the scene of considerable destruction in June 1944. Here, the dance hall blazes after being bombed. The fire spread rapidly to other parts of Tivoli. The sight of Danish teenagers dancing to American swing music had been found offensive by a visiting German Nazi on whose suggestion the hall was destroyed by Danish terrorists.

The group suffered severe losses. John was arrested by the Gestapo after two months. He was hit by seven bullets, one of which broke his right thigh. During the following interrogation the Gestapo agents kicked the fractured leg and bent the lower part of the leg outwards to form a right angle with the upper part. He fainted several times, but he did not talk.

John was betrayed by a woman in whose apartment he found underground accommodation. It became clear to us that informers were one of the greatest threats to the resistance movement. We had to strike back and liquidation of traitors became a necessity which we reluctantly had to accept.

In answer to John's arrest we carried out several actions in Jutland and the action against B&W in Copenhagen. The women

The climax of the fight against the Germans came in late June 1944 when, in response to severe provocations as well as a curfew and restrictions of assembly imposed by the Germans in an effort to curb resistance activity, a "people's strike" was declared. Streets became battle scenes, such as this one, with pavement stones used for barricades. Dr. Best in an outrage at the gall of "this laughing stock of a little country" taking on the mighty Third Reich, closed down approaches to Copenhagen to prevent food supplies from coming in. The Germans shut down water and electricity while awaiting troop reinforcements. Within a week's time, however, they backed down: the curfew and other restrictions were relaxed. It cost the Danes 87 dead and 664 wounded.

who betrayed John escaped to Norway, but when she later returned to Denmark she was shot. By that time John had been executed.

The activities of HD2 suddenly stopped in February 1944 when the group was broken up by the Gestapo after an action against two factories in Aabenraa in Southern Jutland. My friend from Horsens, Peer Borup, was killed, and four members of HD2 were arrested, including my brother Flemming and myself. I was wounded by a bullet in the neck causing a minor fracture of the cervical spine. During the interrogation a blow with the butt of a gun on my head caused a fracture of the skull. When I finally ended up in the German prison in Copenhagen I was in poor shape.

Other members of HD2 escaped to Sweden, but some stayed back, among them Bent Faurschou-Hviid, nicknamed Flammen (the Flame) due to his red hair. Our arrest was due to a traitor, and liquidation of traitors now became Flammen's most important task. When, several months later, he was surrounded by the Germans he took his pill. They did not get him alive.

My two sisters in Copenhagen decided to escape to Sweden. However, just before their departure they were betrayed and arrested. Also my father was arrested in Horsens, leaving my mother and my youngest sister, Lida, as the only members of the family who were not in prison.

Shortly after my arrival in the German prison in Copenhagen I was confronted with John, who was lying on his bed unable to move because of his broken leg. He had not received any medical attention and for almost three months nobody had been allowed to carry him to the toilet or to wash him. Before the confrontation the guards had cleaned his cell and shaved him. However, the expression on his pale face clearly revealed all the hardships he had been through.

I was allowed to visit him several times. We were alone, but we knew of course that the Gestapo was listening. Some of the Germans understood Danish, although they pretended not to. I was also allowed to carry him to the toilet and even out in the prison yard where he enjoyed the sun immensely. We both knew that we would be sentenced to death, but we hoped to be saved by an allied invasion in France or perhaps in Denmark. But gradually the hope faded. "If you can prolong your interrogations you may have a chance," John said to me, "but I am lost."

He was right. In April when I carried him back to his cell from the prison yard they were waiting for him. At the Gestapo headquarters he was sentenced to death, and the following morning at four o'clock I heard the guards opening the door to his cell, which was next to mine. From his letters we know that he asked himself the question: "How are they going to shoot me? I cannot stand!" We don't know how they shot him, but his body was found after the war at the place which is now the Memorial Park of Ryvangen.

The daily interrogations were an extreme psychological strain, but I was not submitted to physical torture. I tried to prolong the case, and I won at the very last moment. In June, the Gestapo had prepared our case for the SS tribunal, but just before the court was assembled it was discovered that the signature of one of my arrested friends on a document of confession was missing. Another group was tried instead. It was the famous Hvidsten group including the innkeper Marius Fiil, his son, his son-in-law, and five more people who had organized the reception and distribution of weapons and explosives sent down by the RAF by parachutes in Northern Jutland. They were all executed the following day.

However, finally it was our turn. Twenty-four hours before the execution a general strike broke out in Copenhagen. The town was put under martial law, and all food and water supplies were cut off. However, the population resisted, and after four nerve-racking days the Germans gave in, and all executions were discontinued for the time being.

Instead, we were deported first to a German camp in Denmark, where I met my father and my oldest sister, and then to Germany, where my brother and I ended up in a concentration camp called Porta Westphalica.

We worked as miners. In order to protect important factories against bombing, the Germans were building underground towns. In the Westphalian mountains we were blasting and digging underground halls, roads, and railroads in seven floors. The longest road was twenty-two kilometers. It was intended to place the Philips factories stolen from Holland in these protected surroundings. The work was never completed but it cost the lives of numerous prisoners. We were about two hundred Danish prisoners in this camp. After six months about half of them were dead including Jørgen Staffeldt who had become the leader of the entire Holger Danske organization after Finn's flight to Sweden. Starvation and tuberculosis were the main causes of death, but physical exhaustion, cold, beatings, and numerous infectious diseases contributed to the high mortality rate.

We all suffered from extreme hunger and experienced severe weight loss, edema, frequent urination, and diarrhea due to the degeneration of the intestinal mucosa. Eventually apathy indicated that the final stage before death—called the Mussulman stage—was approaching. When you could no longer dream, when you could no longer see the faces of your relatives and friends with your internal eye, then you knew that it was only a matter of a few days before your sufferings as a KZ-prisoner had come to an end.

It was at this moment that the Bernadotte expedition saved first the Danish and Norwegian prisoners and later several prisoners from other nations. This help came early enough to save four of the five HD2 saboteurs who had escaped execution and been deported to Germany. But it came too late to save the young student Klaus Rønholt, who had been of enormous encouragement to many of his fellow-prisoners.

After our repatriation we found out, much to our surprise that the whole Kieler family was alive. We were not in good shape, but we were alive. My brother was treated in a hospital for two years before he was cured of the infections he got in Germany. I got contaminated with tuberculosis a week before my repatriation, but I was cured after two years of ambulant treatment.

Other members of HD2 were less successful. One of the cadets, Mix (Erik Koch Michelsen), who had escaped to Sweden, could not stand the life as a refugee while Denmark was still fighting. He returned to Denmark before the end of the war, was caught by the Gestapo, and executed. He deserves particular credit for the successful sabotage of B&W in Copenhagen.

Another of the cadets, Jørgen Salling, who was deported to Porta Westphalica, never recovered from the stress he had been exposed to, and died a few years later. Thus, seven members of HD2 and the leader of the organization, Jørgen Staffeldt, paid the highest price for the right to live as free people irrespective of race and faith and with deep respect for human rights.

NOTE

1. Unlike the situation that prevailed in Denmark, Norway's king and government had called upon its citizens to resist the German invaders for as long as possible. By "Norwegian conditions," then, is meant an open breach with Germany, resignation of the government, and active resistance officially encouraged and sanctioned.

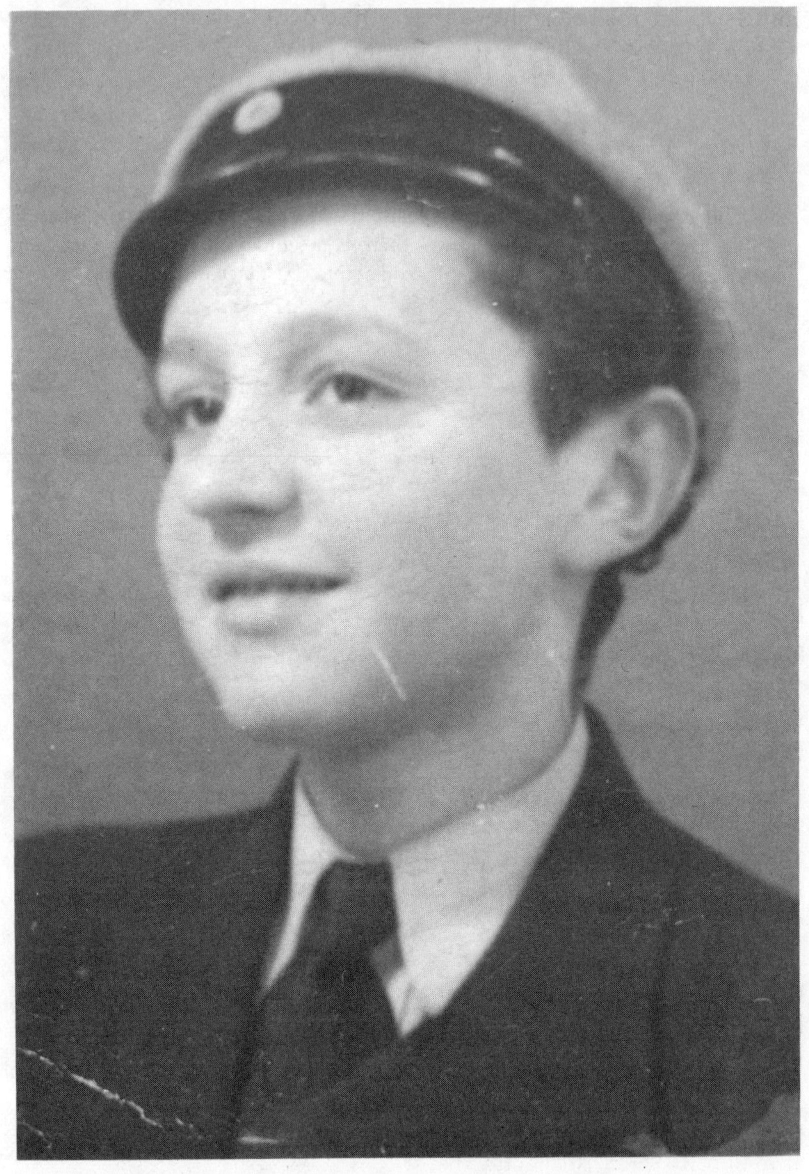

Leo Goldberger as a student in Gothenburg's *Hvitfeldska Läroverket* in Sweden, 1943. He transferred to the Danish refugee school when it was established.

8.

Leo Goldberger

I WILL NEVER FORGET IT. It is still as vivid in my memory as if it were yesterday. The moments of unspeakable terror as well as the kind and warm social support network of the Danes, friends and strangers alike.

I had just had my Bar Mitzvah in June of 1943. Though the luncheon celebration that followed my performance in the synagogue was not as sumptuous as that of my older brother's two years earlier, it was nevertheless a happy event. I even received a few fountain pens, some religious books, and a shiny large police flashlight. Finally to become a "man!" Now perhaps I could do some real resistance work in the underground—not just engage in our childish form of anti-German sentiment: wearing a red, white, and blue cap or lapel pin, pinching a German soldier in a crowded street then running like the devil, pouring sugar in the gas tank of a German car, and the like.

With my parents and my two brothers, we had moved in 1934 to Denmark from Troppau (in the Moravian part of Czechoslovakia) where my father had been serving as chief cantor. (He and my mother had originally come from Bratislava, Slovakia, and had settled in Troppau, a prosperous and comfortable Jewish community in Moravia.) Albeit a restless person, my father had sensed anti-Semitism in the air and cast about for a new position and a

First published in Carol Rittner and Sondra Myers, eds., *The Courage to Care: Rescuers of Jews During the Holocaust* (New York: New York University Press, 1986). (Reprinted by permission)

new country. It may have been a Nazi parade here and a German nationalistic slogan there, not to mention direct anti-Semitic remarks that made my father want out, despite all assurances by his many friends and fellow Jews in Troppau that he was imagining things. By chance, really, there was a vacancy for the prestigious cantorial position in Copenhagen's Great Synagogue. He applied, tried out for it, and was appointed. Moving—furniture, grand piano, and all—we quickly were settled in the picturesque old center of town, integrated into the cozy Danish way of life, learned the language and its customs, and felt very much at home there. There was not a hint of anti-Semitism. Jews had achieved a large share of their civil rights way back in 1814 (and total equality in 1849) generations ago, and had over the years earned a highly respected place in all walks of life.

Then came the fateful day, 9 April 1940. The widening scope of the war hit our beautiful, little, and avowedly neutral land—and it had only recently signed a nonagression pact with the Germans. The early morning sky was blackened by roaring low-flying planes. From my window I reached out to catch a green leaflet coming down from the sky like confetti. In comical, broken Danish the leaflet appealed to all Danes to remain calm. The German *Wehrmacht* had no aggressive intentions, they only wanted to protect us from the evil designs of the Allies. We were urged to go about our daily business as usual—as if nothing had happened. And, indeed, after an emotionally moving appeal on the radio by the prime minister and our beloved old king—Christian X—we did just that. Life went on—Tivoli remained open, the king rode his horse daily through the busy streets in his usual routine, and government, police, and army remained in place with no external evidence of anything unusual having happened, except that we had a lot of armed "guests"—soldiers, airmen, naval and S.S. personnel not to mention tanks—all over the place. It was like a gothic Hans Christian Andersen tale. It was unreal. In retrospect, it seems even odder to realize that Jewish life also went on as usual—Jewish clubs, the synagogue, the Jewish school, which I attended—all functioned as usual. Well, maybe not exactly as usual. There was an air of tense, ominous anticipation of what might be in store next, an uneasiness that was particularly strong among those in the

At the beginning of the occupation, life went on more or less as usual. Jews were in no way subject to special conditions or restrictions; they were fully protected under Danish law. Any German interference was discouraged very strongly by the Danish governement. Despite the ominous presence of the *Wehrmacht* and war-zone preparations, a sense of normalcy and calm prevailed. Here Leo Goldberger, as a youngster in 1940, is seen with his father against the backdrop of a freshly dug air-raid shelter in Copenhagen.

Jewish community, like my father, who along with many Jews with Eastern European roots, had already experienced pogroms of one kind or another.

During the first years of the German occupation the Danish resistance movement was rather small, numbering no more than some three thousand in a country of four and a half million. With the help of the Allies and their secret air drops the Resistance grew better organized, effective, and menacing—having evolved from publishing and distributing illegal newsletters to massive sabotage and bombings of strategic war-related factories and rail tracks. This was more than the Germans had bargained for. To them, Danes were an affable, apolitical peasant people, and though freedom-loving and strong-headed, they were easily handled as long as they were not irritated or provoked too much by display of authority. The very mention of the so-called Jewish problem was an obvious irritant to the Danes—it was none of the Germans' business. It was not to be pursued. At least not right at the start. Yet, the infernal problem of the saboteurs had to be dealt with firmly.

The Germans issued an ultimatum in August 1943. The Danish government authorities had to see to it that all saboteurs were handed the death penalty. Other encroachments on Danish judicial and governmental autonomy were also at issue. The government refused to give in to the ultimatum—and all hell broke loose. Leaders representing all walks of life were arrested as hostages. My father, as a functionary of the Jewish community, was among those on the list to be arrested.

It was the night of 28 August, around three o'clock in the morning—I was awakened by loud rings and knocks on our front door. It sounded like rifle butts against the door and the heavy metalic footsteps of soldiers. My father quickly came in to my brother's and my room and whispered that the Germans were outside and that he would not under any circumstances open the door. For me, this was the most terror-filled moment I had ever experienced. The insistent loud knocks of rifle butts. Fearing that they would break down the door any minute, I implored my father to open it, but he was determined not to. Then in the nick of time, we heard our upstairs neighbor's voice telling the German soldiers that we—the Goldbergers—were away for the summer, and that three o'clock in the morning was in any case no time to make such a racket! They posted a guard outside our apartment building which we could see through our curtains. We first hid in the bomb shelter entered by the back stairs and then snuck out the back way some twenty-four hours later with my father in disguise—he had shaven off his Vandyke in order to look less conspicuous. We hastened to the train and headed out of town, my father's face burrowed in a newspaper. It had been his fortieth birthday, 28 August. Some birthday!

We joined the rest of the family—my mother and baby brother—who were, indeed, in our rented summer home on the coast near Elsinore. My father had foiled the Germans; he had not become a hostage! By mid-September my parents decided that things had cooled down enough for us to return to our Copenhagen apartment. After all, my brothers and I had to continue with school, and my father had to prepare for the High Holyday services. But there were even more threatening events to come in the next weeks.

The crisis that had begun in early August had reached its climax on 29 August. The government had stood its ground and finally had chosen to resign en masse. An entirely new situation in the German-Danish relationship took shape. No more pretense of who ran the show. It was clearly the Germans now who were in power. The king was under guard at his summer palace. The army was stripped, demobilized. Officers were placed in detention camps along with the hostages. The police and coast guard no longer thought it their duty to carry out anything other than clearly nonpolitical, domestic functions—which excluded apprehending saboteurs or, for that matter, people escaping to Sweden.

Though the idea of escaping to Sweden had rarely surfaced as a viable option before—it was considered almost impossible because of heavy patrols, Danish as well as German—the time was getting close at hand at least to try. The clock was ticking away. Then suddenly the explicit warning came: the Germans were about to round us all up and send us off to a concentration camp. The time was now more than ripe to escape. The warning came near the end of September from a courageous German in the high command's office in Copenhagen—Naval Counselor G. F. Duckwitz. It was forwarded to the Jews through Danish intermediaries and announced on the morning of Wednesday, 29 September, the day before Rosh Hashana in the synagogue by the rabbi. We were urged to go into hiding at least temporarily, and to spread the word to all other Jews not in the synagogue that morning. The German action was to take place during Rosh Hashana, between Friday night and Saturday 1 and 2 October, when most Jews were to be at home celebrating the solemn Jewish new year, if not the Sabbath.

Where to hide? Our first night was spent as guests of a wealthy Jewish family who lived on the coast about thirty-five minutes from Copenhagen. To our chagrin the family took off for Sweden during the night, without even telling us or their German-Jewish refugee maid. Apparently my father had been asked by our host whether he wanted to share in the expense of chartering a Cris Craft to take us all to Sweden but had declined. He simply did not have that kind of money. Near panic but determined to find a way somehow, my father took the train back to the city; he needed to borrow money, perhaps get an advance on his salary, and see about making contacts for passage on a fishing boat. As luck would have it, on the train a Christian woman whom he knew only slightly recognized him and inquired about his obviously agitated state. He confided our plight. Without a moment's hesitation the lady promised to take care of everything. She would meet my father at the main railroad station with all the information about the arrangements within a few hours. It was the least she could do, she said, in return for my father's participation some years back in a benefit concert for her organization—the Women's League for Peace and Freedom, a group of Danish women who already in the thirties began relief work.

True to her word, she met my father later that day and indicated that all was arranged. The money would be forthcoming from a Pastor Henry Rasmussen (a Lutheran minister associated with the Israel Mission). The sum was a fairly large one—about 20,000 kronen, 5,000 per person (the equivalent of about $3,500 in all, which to my father was an enormous amount at the time). And though it was ostensibly a loan, I should add that Pastor Rasmussen refused repayment after the war. The next step was for all of us

Fanny Arnskov, who was a leading figure in the Women's League for Peace and Freedom, played a significant role in helping Jews during the days of the rescue and later took charge of sending parcels to the Danish Jews in Theresienstadt. She was in all likelihood the "kind angel" on the train who recognized and helped Cantor Goldberger in his most desperate moment of need.

A young Danish Jew upon his arrival in Sweden escorted by a Swedish policeman. The refugees were warmly welcomed by the Swedes whose foreign policy had just begun to undergo a shift to a pro-Allied stance. The refugees—including some fourteen thousand Danish non-Jews also on the run from the Germans—were permitted to find work, to live on their own rather than in camps, to form their own schools, and even to establish a military brigrade for the eventual liberation of Denmark.

to head for a certain address near the coast, less than an hour from Copenhagen. After hurriedly getting some things together from our apartment—a few clothes, some treasured papers and family photos, and, in my case, my newly acquired police flashlight, we were off by taxi to our unknown hosts for the night and our uncertain destiny.

The following night we were standing, huddled in some low bushes along the beach in Dragør, an outskirt of Copenhagen's island of Amager. It was a bitter cold October night. My youngest

The Danish refugees established their own social enclaves in several major cities in Sweden where many quickly found suitable employment and places to live. They even formed their own, albeit improvised, school system (with the help of the Danish Embassy) in which the standard Danish curriculum was taught using texts from Denmark. Here is the class from the Danish School in Gothenburg that Leo Goldberger attended through May 1945 (he may be seen standing in the back row at the far left; Salli Besiakov, who drew the map for this volume, is sitting to the left of the teacher). Some of the two hundred students in the school were the sons and daughters of Danish resistance fighters forced to flee when things got too dangerous for them in Denmark. The school was run by a colorful array of teachers and visiting examiners who included such noted academics as Professors Harold Bohr, Franz Blatt, and Lektor Aage Bertelsen—themselves refugees.

brother, barely three years old, had been given a sleeping pill to keep him quiet. My brave and stoic little mother was clutching her bag with socks and stockings to be mended that she took along for reasons difficult to fathom rationally. We were anxiously and eagerly waiting for the promised light signal. As we were poised to move toward the signal, I could not help but wonder *why* this was

In better days! A sumptuous prewar wedding party at the Bjalle's at which a number of the Jewish community's functionnairies were present. Seated at the left, Rabbi and Mrs. Max Friediger; seated at the right, Cantor and Mrs. Eugene Goldberger; standing in the back (left) Cantor Leo Grabowski and on the far right, Julius Kaminkowitz, Hebrew teacher and assistant cantor. The chief sexton, Herman Margolinsky and his wife are the second couple standing on the right.

all happening. What had we ever done to be in hiding, escaping like criminals? Where would it all end? And why in God's name did the signal not appear? Then finally the lights flashed. We were off! Wading straight into the sea, we walked out some one hundred feet through icy water, in water that reached up to my chest. My father carried my two small brothers on his arm. My mother held on to her bag of socks. And I clutched my precious flashlight. My older brother tried valiantly to carry the suitcases but finally had to let them drop in the water. We were hauled aboard the boat, directed in whispers to lie concealed in the cargo area, there to stretch out covered by smelly canvases; in the event German patrols were to inspect the boat, we would be passed over as fish. There seemed to have been some twenty other Jews aboard. As we proceeded out toward the open sea my father chanted a muted prayer from the Psalms. A few hours later—bright lights appeared along the coastal outline of Sweden. Wonderful, peaceful, Sweden. A welcoming haven where we remained until our return to Denmark at the conclusion of the war in 1945. Our apartment and belongings had been left undisturbed, ready for us to resume our lives among our many Danish friends.

How can I ever forget? How can I ever stop mulling it over, wondering about the whys and wherefores? The Danes were truly fantastic. No doubt about it. Our neighbor upstairs, on the night they came to arrest my father, was great. The lady on the train was an angel. Pastor Rasmussen, a true Christian. The fisherman, though he charged a good penny—he was, after all, diverted from fishing to the transportation business—*did* risk his life; he was a courageous, yes a noble soul. And there were thousands of others all across Denmark who helped and cared, tending to us—some 7200 as it turned out, who succeeded in our escape, out of a total of some 7,800 Jews. What a magnificent feat! And to think that for the Danes the rescue seemed only natural. Not a big deal. Not something for which recognition ought to be accorded. For them it was the only way. Yet in my mind their deed remains a moral object lesson of how we all ought to behave in the face of injustice and suffering. Their example puts the "innocent bystanders"—so prevalent throughout the Holocaust years—to shame.

MORAL COURAGE UNDER STRESS

9.

INTRODUCTION TO THE CONFERENCE "MORAL CHOICE UNDER STRESS"

RABBI MARC H. TANENBAUM

THOSE OF US who have been concerned for many years about the meaning of the Nazi Holocaust—its significance to the Jewish people and to mankind at large—have been preoccupied with trying to learn lessons from how that evil could come to be. How could it have happened in a country of ancient Christian civilization, a land that prided itself on the most advanced science and technology? How could it have become such a murderous killing machine which sought to liquidate the entire Jewish people? Perforce we have found ourselves together with an increasing number of Christian friends and colleagues studying the psychopathology of the human condition.

To preserve our sense of hope in human survival, it is essential to understand not only psychopathology but also those manifestations that are affirmation of life, not simply the destruction of life.

In 1954, I had the privilege of organizing an event in honor of two high-school teachers from Aarhus, Denmark, Aage Bertelsen and his wife. These teachers, when they learned that their Jewish neighbors were about to be transported to destruction in Germany, Poland, Auschwitz, or Theresienstadt, alone organized an underground network where they, together with others in the Danish community, helped save at least eight hundred Jews, ferrying them across to Sweden.

Aage Bertelsen wrote a book, *October 43,*[1] which is an account of what happened, what happened to him, what led him together with virtually the entire Danish people—from the king down to the simplest fisherman—to mobilize their entire society to save almost the entire Jewish community. He invited Sholom Asch to write the foreword to his American edition of his book, part of which follows:

> Let me state at the outset that this book, *October 43,* deals with one of the unhappiest chapters in modern history of mankind. Nevertheless, it is not a sad book, but a joyous one, a book not of human degradation, but of human exultation, for it is a book not of hatred, but of the noblest form of love which man is capable of demonstrating. I would call it the book of the greatest psalm of praise, an ode to the human species. Between these two covers are lodged the hopes and the comfort which sustain you and me and sustain all mankind. You and I need the word of comfort, of hope, of faith in man.

If one looks about the world, one could respond with an incredible sense of paralysis and hopelessness. There is not a continent on the earth today where human beings, in that legacy of evil, are not massacring, torturing, killing other human beings—Afghanistan, Poland, Uganda, Ethiopia, Southeast Asia, Meskito Indians and Nicaragua, Guatemala. One could despair. Who would want to raise children in a world that is so demonically obsessed? And yet somehow it is essential for the human spirit to recognize that side by side with these tragedies and destruction of the human life are redeeming moments and models of human caring and love and sacrifice and compassion. Nowhere in recent human history has that been more powerfully, more dramatically exemplified for us than by the experience of the 8,000 Jews in Denmark, 7,200 of whom survived as the result of the caring and the love and the human solidarity, the affirmation of life that both Danish moral tradition and democratic tradition fused together to affirm.

REFERENCE

Bertelsen, Aage, *October 1943*. New York: Putnam, 1954.

10.

GRUNDTVIG'S INFLUENCE

JAROSLAV PELIKAN

LET ME BEGIN with an anecdote from a Danish friend of mine. She is now a handsome and stately matron, with exquisite taste in language, clothes, and food. But in October 1943 she was, she recalled, "a hopeless tomboy, with scratches on my knees and stains on my clothes from climbing trees." Into her rather comfortable family home there was introduced a family of refugees, who had emigrated from Vienna to Copenhagen after *Anschluss*. Included in that family was a girl of about her own age, but one who was, in utter contrast to my friend's "tomboy" demeanor, "already a total lady," dignified in her silk stockings and inpeccably correct deportment. It must have seemed strange to be told on the Nazi-controlled Danish radio that such a creature belonged to an inferior race! Fearing for the safety of their guests, the family did not even inform their servants that someone was hiding in the attic. Instead, they feigned enormous hunger, requesting enough food at each meal for themselves and for the invisible diners. Finally they were able to smuggle the Jews out to Sweden in an apple cart. Years later, when the war was over, my friend recalled, the daughter of the refugee family invited her to the best restaurant in Copenhagen for an elegant meal, to reciprocate, as the sometime refugees explained, the guest-friendship they had received in October 1943. My friend concluded her story with the plea that we not romanticize the events of that month, for that is not what the

Danes would want: How could they have done anything other than what they did?

The year 1983 of the Common Era marked the five hundredth birthday of Martin Luther. Martin Luther—who, in Heinrich Heine's memorable phrase, "could scold like a fishwife [and] could also be as gentle as a sensitive maiden"[1]—found it possible to speak about Judaism and about Jews with a coarseness that sometimes went well beyond the vulgar anti-Semitism of his time. It is not, thank God, my assignment to examine the historical reasons for this. They have been well analyzed in a recent book by Professor Heiko Oberman of Tübingen, entitled *Roots of Anti-Semitism,* soon to appear in English translation.[2] Rather, I want to address myself to a less depressing, but no less intriguing, question: Why should it have been that forty years ago this month the Lutherans of Denmark, no less Luther's spiritual descendants than were the Lutherans of Germany, manifested the moral heroism and humane courage for which we are paying tribute to them today?

As part of the historical answer to this question I want to consider another anniversary marked in 1983. When I was in Denmark in April 1983 as guest lecturer at the universities of Copenhagen and Aarhus, that anniversary was being observed at both universities: the two hundredth birthday of Nikolai F. S. Grundtvig (1783–1872). In his long and remarkable life, Grundtvig laid the foundations of the Danish folk school, provided the inspiration for the cooperative movement, and wrote more than a thousand hymns. For me, as a medievalist, it is significant that, in Kemp Malone's words,[3] "the first and greatest of *Beowulf* scholars, as everybody knows, was N. F. S. Grundtvig. . . . Of the many scholars who have followed Grundtvig in the field, none can compare with him in genius or in importance of achievement."[4] Above all, however, he was the fountainhead of a "Christian humanism" whose literary flower we can find in the writings of Kaj Munk[5] and whose moral fruit we can find in the events of October 1943. At the very outset of my discussion of Grundtvig, let me acknowledge my debt to a splendid Danish essay entitled "Grundtvig's Challenge to Modern Theology," by my colleague, Professor Regin Prenter of the University of Aarhus.[6]

As the most confessedly Lutheran of German Lutherans has put

N. F. S. Grundtvig (1783–1872), the greatest spiritual force in Denmark's history, whose life was devoted to the enlightenment of the common people and to civil and religious freedom. His work, which brought him into frequent doctrinal conflict with the established Lutheran church, was preserved in the founding of the folk high school. He emphasized the study of national history and literature; his influence is apparent in many of the psalms and hymns that are still sung today. The revival of the Grundtvigian blend of spiritual nationalism undoubtedly played a significant role in Denmark's opposition to German oppression and injustice.

it, "Grundtvig is the quintessential Dane (*Grundtvig aber ist der Däne schlechthin*). . . . For except for Luther himself, there is no one who has so consciously and so successfully made the national expression of the Church of the Reformation the very content of his lifework (*Wirkung*) as he did."[7] That "national expression" is still visible in many aspects of Danish cultural life, as lectures and articles commemorating the Grundtvig bicentennial have been pointing out. But the presence of Grundtvig also helps us to understand the rescue of the Danish Jews. The special connection between Grundtvig's Lutheran Christianity and Grundtvig's Danish nationality means that we should not, in the strict sense, speak about "Danish Jews," but about "Jewish Danes." As a recent study has shown,[8] the widespread European pattern of assimilation, especially in the aftermath of the Haskalah, took a special form in Denmark: Jews there were granted equality in the Danish constitution of 1849, with access to the university, to commercial opportunity, and to social status. The very qualities of the Danish "folk church" to which Søren Kierkegaard made such eloquent objection—because they obscured any sharp distinction between being "Danish" and being "Christian"—meant, in this instance, that Danish citizens who did not attend the Lutheran state church because they were Jewish suffered from no more significant handicaps than did their unbelieving Gentile compatriots, who also did not go to church.

Yet there were many Jews in Germany during the late eighteenth and nineteenth centuries who believed that their status, as totally acculturated and assimilated members of the society, was no less assured. The archives and lectures of the Leo Baeck Institute in New York are replete with case studies of scholars and writers, artists and businessmen, who had grown up believing that whatever remaining problems there were between Gentile Germans and Jewish Germans were in the process of being solved. Christian Germans, whether Protestant or Roman Catholic, likewise spoke as though these problems had, at least in principle, been overcome. The tragic betrayal of such beliefs is the most overpowering event in the history of the twentieth century. Therefore one must ask again: How was the Danish situation different? The extremely important social and political reasons for the difference I must leave to others; but as a historian of ideas, I would suggest that at least part of the answer must be sought in the thought of Grundtvig, including his recognition, as a recent study has put it, that although "he wanted to perform his work in the spirit of Martin Luther," he could not do what Luther did, because "neither the situation nor the problems of his day were the same as those of the sixteenth century."[9] Let me mention, with far greater brevity than either the importance of the topic of the present state of research would warrant, several features of his thought that seem pertinent.

To begin at the beginning, *b'reeshith,* Grundtvig "has," in the words of the late great Danish church historian Hal Koch, "taken the creation idea seriously: man . . . is a divine experiment."[10] On the basis of my lifelong study of the history of Christian doctrine, I am convinced that the doctrine of creation has always been dependent on the Christian awareness of the Hebrew Bible. Although the New Testament, almost all of which was written by Jews, is of course replete with allusions to that doctrine, most of them are in fact echoes of what Christians came to call the Old Testament—or, as I prefer to say, the "Original and Basic" Testament. Nevertheless, the conflict with the heretic Marcion in the second century demonstrated that a denial of the Hebrew Bible and a rejection of creation went hand in hand. Conversely, those periods in the history of Christian doctrine in which creation has been central have also been times when the mythology and the very language of the Book of Genesis have been prominent. Grundtvig's rediscovery of the basic emphasis on the doctrine of creation was expressed in the familiar motto: "First a human being, then a Christian: this alone is life's order."[11] This was a rejection of the notion, which had become current in certain forms of Lutheran Pietism, that the doctrine of creation could take second place in the scale of Christian teachings, since it belonged to "natural theology" and therefore was not part of specifically Christian revelation. On the contrary, Grundtvig insisted, God the Redeemer was God the Creator first, and therefore it was not permissible to speak about redemption until and unless one had first affirmed what the Christian creeds all affirmed: "I believe in God the Father, the Creator."

Now if that is taken to be true, an immediate and ineluctable corollary is that all those who have been the objects of the love of

Hal Koch (1904–1963), professor of theology, played a key role in the first years of the occupation through his fiery public lectures, which aimed to arouse national unity and reinforced democratic ideals. He lectured on historical parallels to earlier periods in Denmark's history, highlighting Grundtvig's place in the Danish national consciousness. He adamantly opposed such anti-Democratic notions as special legislation for Jews. Though critical of the government he was not a member of the active resistance movement, choosing to remain neutral rather than join its opposition to the politicians.

God the Creator are bound to one another with ties more profound than any of the barriers that human history, including the history of religion, may have constructed. Therefore there is a kind of "pre-Christian ecumenicity," by which I must have a kinship to all those who may lay claim to the name "human," before I may claim a kinship with all those who name the name of Jesus Christ. Much of Christian history has, God knows, lost sight even of "Christian ecumenicity," shared between those who do name the name of Christ. But before and beneath that, there is an ecumenicity without which Christian fellowship is clannish and "clubby." Because Christian history has so often neglected this, Grundtvig's insight is of fundamental importance. His chapter on "Israel's Church-State" in his *Handbook of History*[12] demonstrates that, in the words of Henning Høirup, "it is characteristic of Grundtvig as a historian of the church that he views the later relation of Christianity to the various nations in the light of the history of Israel."[13] And because Christians have forgotten this especially in relation to that history of those with whom they shared the most, including the Hebrew Bible and the community of Israel from which Jesus sprang, the presence of that insight in the Danish Christian tradition is basic.

Like Tolstoy and Dostoevsky, Grundtvig and Kierkegaard were contemporaries who were born to be contrasted. Kierkegaard expressed, with unique power, the recognition that each person is individually accountable before God; but Grundtvig recognized, with a profundity that was born of the Hebrew Bible but that was rare among nineteenth-century Protestant Christians, that the imperatives of biblical faith are not individualistic.[14] As has been pointed out, however, "Søren Kierkegaard shared completely Grundtvig's outlook on 'the national,' "[15] but spoke as though the summons of the Gospel invited one to an individual acceptance of divine grace, which was unique in relation to the natural awareness of creation. On the contrary, Grundtvig urged, in the words of one of his many hymns,[16]

> Growth springs alive as good tidings arrive,
> Harvest will come on the morrow;
> Power and nerve, a commitment to serve,

Comfort and hope in all sorrow.
Gently the Gospel fulfills its task;
Mercy is given to all who ask.

Therefore when God calls any one of us into fellowship with Him, it is into community that we are called. As a friend (who is also, incidentally, the translator of the poetry of Grundtvig that I just quoted) put it, altogether in the Grundtvigian spirit, "there must be a vital force which motivates, which binds, which sustains, and which renews the community, and this means the community of man with God, the community of man with man, and the community of man with the created world. . . . That force," he concluded, "must be integral to religion, and without it there can be neither religion nor community."[17]

Behind all of this is the most fundamental of all insights, be they religious or metaphysical or even political: the oneness of God. We who stand in the Judaeo-Christian tradition tend to take it for granted, though everything in the history of both our communities militates against our taking it for granted. It was, and is, a colossal act of metaphysical audacity to declare that all the multifarious and indeed heterogeneous elements of our experience, and of reality itself, are nevertheless single in their origin and therefore ultimately single in their meaning. The fundamental and normative statements of faith of our two communities both affirm this: *Shema' Yisrael, Hashshem Elohenu Hashshem echad; Credo in unum Deum*. Acceptance of this creed does not automatically produce a sense of a common bond, as both the history of the Crusades and the history of the modern Near East tragically demonstrate. Nevertheless, without that common bond it is difficult to understand how Jews and Christians (and Muslims) can ever find a foundation for mutual understanding. And it was the historic accomplishment of Grundtvig to have seen again that there can be no Christian community and no Christian dogma and no Christian morality without the *Shema*.

Having begun with an anecdote from 1943, I close with a joke and a book from that same period. It was a most remarkable book, by Gustaf Aulén, the Swedish scholar and bishop to whose most important theological book, *Christus Victor,* I had the privilege of writing a foreword in 1969. In the official bibliography of the works of Bishop Aulén,[18] there is one title that seems rather strange if one knew the author: *Andagtbog for Hjem og Skole,* published in Copenhagen in 1944. But the bibliography goes on to explain: "An illegal publication (*Illegalt tryck*)." For inside the jacket of this *Book of Devotions for Home and School,* which was on sale in Copenhagen throughout World War II and the occupation, was in fact a book entitled *Kirken og Nationalsocialismen,* warning against the threat of national socialism to authentic Christian faith. Bishop Aulén, who lived to be nearly ninety, could not speak of this Danish book without a chuckle: Why would any Nazi suppose that a devotional book was a threat? And yet it was, for the God to whom it was addressed and dedicated was the sovereign Lord of heaven and earth, from whose justice no nation could finally escape.

Through the Danes the Lord of heaven and earth managed to play the kind of cosmic joke that Grundtvig has taught us to appreciate, a joke from which all of us can learn. And so perhaps the last word belongs, as it should, to the psalmist: "He that sitteth in the heavens shall laugh. The LORD shall have them in derision."

NOTES

1. Heinrich Heine, *Religion and Philosophy in Germany: A Fragment,* tr. John Snodgrass (Boston: Beacon Press, 1959), p. 46.

2. Heiko A. Oberman, *Wurzeln des Antisemitismus: Christenangst und Judenplage im Zeitalter von Humanismus und Reformation* (Berlin: Severin und Siedler, 1981), pp. 125–83.

3. Kemp Malone, "Grundtvig as *Beowulf* Critic," *Review of English Studies* 17 (1941):129.

4. Cf. the comparison of Grundtvig with other scholars, including J. R. R. Tolkien, by Andreas Haarder, "Grundtvigs vurdering af Beowulf som kunstværk," *Grundtvig-Studier* (1963):7–36.

5. Kaj Munk (1898–1944) was a celebrated playwright. His opposition to the Nazis led to his brutal murder, mourned throughout the country.

6. Regin Prenter, "Grundtvigs udfordring til moderne theologi," *Grundtvig-Studier* (1973):11–29.

7. Werner Elert, *Morphologie des Luthertums* (2 vols.; Munich: C.H. Beck, 1931–32), 2:244.

8. Ib Nathan Bamberger, *A Cultural History of the Jews of Denmark, 1622–1900* (D. H. L. dissertation, Yeshiva University), University Microfilms, 1974.

9. Ernest D. Nielsen, "N. F. S. Grundtvig on Luther," *Interpreters of Luther: Essays in Honor of Wilhelm Pauck,* ed. by Jaroslav Pelikan (Philadelphia: Fortress, 1968), p. 184.

10. Hal Koch, *Grundtvig,* tr. Llewellyn Jones (Yellow Springs: Antioch College Press, Ohio, 1952), p. 157.

11. Harry Aronson, *Mänskligt och Kristet: En studie i Grundtvigs teologi* (Stockholm: Svenska Bokförlaget, 1960), esp. pp. 15–23.

12. N. F. S. Grundtvig, *Haandbog i Verdens-Historien* (1833), *Udvalgte Skrifter,* ed. H. Begtrup (10 vols.; Copenhagen: Gyldendal, 1904–09), 5:107–24.

13. Henning Høirup, "Grundtvigs Gedanken über Christentum und Volk," *Grundtvig-Studier* (1952):73.

14. Harry Aronson, *Mänskligt och Kristet,* op. cit. pp. 272–93:

15. Carl Weltzer, *Grundtvig og Søren Kierkegaard* (Copenhagen: Gyldendal, 1952), p. 51.

16. "Spirit of God, Sent from Heaven Abroad," tr. Johannes H. V. Knudsen, *Lutheran Book of Worship* (Minneapolis and Philadelphia: Augsberg and Fortress Presses, 1978), # 285, stanza 3.

17. Johannes H. V. Knudsen, *Called Out of Chaos* (Chicago: Lutheran School of Theology at Chicago Press, 1971), p. 46.

18. Krister Gierow, *Bibliografi over Gustaf Auléns tryckta skrifter* (Lund: C.W.K. Gleerup, 1959).

11.

A PSYCHOLOGICAL PERSPECTIVE

Otto F. Kernberg

In what follows I am offering a psychoanalytic theory to explain, at least in part, the extraordinary behavior of an extraordinary people during what was one of the darkest periods of human history. The theory has to do with the psychoanalytic understanding of the psychology of groups.

In 1921 Freud, in *Group Psychology and the Analysis of the Ego,* published the first psychoanalytic study of group processes. He suggested that members of large crowds[1] who follow a leader by identifying both with each other and with the leader, obtain a sense of power greater than the sense of power each would experience individually. The leader serves each member of the group as an ideal figure. The crowd thus acquires a sense of being free from moral responsibility and exultantly expresses ordinarily suppressed impulses, particularly its aggression against some collectively agreed-upon target under the direction of the leader.

Years later Wilfred Bion[2] and others studied the psychology of small groups—ten to twelve people—whose only task was to sit in a circle and talk to each other about whatever came into their minds and to observe themselves as they did so. The sessions lasted for somewhere between an hour and an hour and a half. Then Kenneth Rice[3] and Pierre Turquet[4] applied the same procedure to larger groups of 60, 80, and even up to 150 people, groups again unstructured in the sense of being held together not by a concrete task related to their environment but merely by talking at random and by self-observation.

The results of these experiments were remarkable. Within minutes the members, regardless of their psychological health or emotional maturity, fell into a primitive emotional state. In a word, they regressed. It is generally agreed that the only recourse for avoiding this regression was for the individual members to withdraw from the group or to join with other members to accomplish some task that linked them to their environment.

In essence, in small groups, there is a tendency to form what Bion called the "fight-flight" group, the "dependent" group, and the "pairing" group, referring to group situations in which primitive emotions take over, rationality and the sense of time tend to get lost, individuals experience themselves as unskilled, and the group sways under various dominant emotions.

In the fight-flight group there is a tendency to search for external enemies, a sense that security only lies in grouping together and fighting off such enemies, sometimes in the form of an internal split of the group in which the enemy is an inside subgroup. A paranoid fighter is the ideal leader of this group. In the dependency group, in contrast, the group spirit is one of helplessness; only a "messianic leader," who is totally self-assured can tell them what to do, and the idealization and greedy expectation from such a nurturant leader replaces the ordinary capacity for rational action on the part of all the members.

And, finally, in the pairing group, there is an effort to escape from the painful emotional experiences of the fight-flight or dependent group in the search for sexual excitement and gratification symbolized by the intimacy of one couple, heterosexual or homosexual, that concentrates the interest of the entire group around it.

Under task-oriented leadership, in contrast, the same feelings of wanting to stand together to fight for the group, of following the idealized leader in carrying out the task, may bring about an intense dedication to the task and a capacity for altruism and self-sacrifice at the service of love and creativity, rather than hatred and destruction.

Under conditions of regression in large unstructured groups of, say, 100 to 150 people, in the sway of the primitive emotions I have mentioned, what also emerges is a general fear of aggression, coupled with direct expression of aggression of part of the group, and a general irritability.

One outcome of group regression is the emergence of what may be called a narcissistic leader. Members of the group whose narcissism drives them to look for power and prestige find favor with the group, which, in its state of regression, approves of the sort of simplistic, vague, cliché-ridden ideas such narcissistic personalities are wont to offer. The large unstructured group finds such ideas soothing: it becomes static, self-satisfied, and its violence evaporates.

Freud's suggestion that the leader of the crowd is one who stimulates his followers to join him in a violent struggle against external enemies has to be complemented with the concept of this other, narcissistic, leader. In contrast to what we might call the "paranoid" leader of the violent mob, we have the soothing leader of the self-satisfied, self-contained, "narcissistic" group. The paranoid and narcissistic leaders have in common the high degree of irrationality, the elimination of a sense of personal moral responsibility and of independent judgment of the reality the group faces.

Didier Anzieu[5] and Janine Chasseguet-Smirgel[6] have described the temptation within small unstructured groups to escape from the conflicts around aggression by means of religiously tinged fantasies that, as long as every member maintains his loyalty to that group, the world is in order, everybody in the group is equal to all other members, all differences—even those between the sexes—are erased; the group is self-engendered (as if it were its own mother), and it will provide solutions for all frustrations and unhappiness. This grandiose narcissistic quality is similar to the atmosphere that prevails in the narcissistic larger group.

Usually, this kind of group spirit is also strongly opposed to any kind of authority. The regressive group has, in psychoanalytic terms, the mentality of a very young infant whose sole aim is self-gratification and denial of reality, an infant not yet mature enough to recognize and subject itself to the rational authority of its parents.

Before I can properly address the question regarding the behavior of the Danish people in saving the Danish Jews, I must add a few more words about leaders of groups and about ideology.

A single ideology can serve a variety of purposes, depending on how it is presented by leaders and also depending on the emotional state of the groups to whom it is presented. Take, for example, Marxism. Originally an attempt to be a scientific theory of economics and politics, the aspect having to do with exploitation of the working class lends itself to be taken up by ambitious, power-hungry, "paranoid" leaders so that it appeals to groups who are in a state of regression characterized by the dominance of paranoid ideas and feelings of omnipotence—the leftist terrorist groups of Europe or Latin America, for example.

The same ideology, with its affirmation of universal equality, its promise of the withering away of the state (implying a denial of aggression), also lends itself to becoming an ideology of universal love and a shedding of individual responsibility. Such an ideology—characterized by narcissism and grandiosity—represents the counterpart to the previous one. It appealed to the counterculture during the sixties.

And the same ideology of Marxism, dominating the Soviet Union and its satellites, has become diluted and trivial and literally largely devoid of its original meaning. It would seem to me fair to assume that the Soviet Union and its satellites contain few "true believers" and that "Marxism" is generally accepted as a conventional system of cultural conformity, necessary for survival in these totalitarian states.

Yet there are versions of Marxism that do not fall into any of the categories I have described. Some parts of Marxist theory have long since been incorporated in the social-democratic ideologies of the Scandinavian countries, as an example. This version of Marxism is rational rather than doctrinaire; it recognizes individuals and individual responsibility; its appeal is to the middle-of-the-roaders, and it is transmitted to them by rational, task-oriented leaders.

So much for the theory. Now to apply it to the case in point, the collective rescue operation in Denmark.

From all we know, the Danish resistance movement presented a highly effective, rational leadership to a society long accustomed to a humanistic ideology, never tempted by extremes of either left or right. The assault, onto such a community, of the primitive, paranoid ideology of the Nazi invaders; the internalization of profound ethical convictions as part of Denmark's culture and religion; and the maintenance of common links of the entire community in contrast to regressive "splitting off" of Jews as a rejected subgroup of that culture, may jointly provide the explanation of why conditions existed under which individual courage and heroism as well as the collective courage of a community was possible.

The Danish people had a long history of parliamentary democracy, a constitutional monarchy and an elected political leadership that worked effectively with both the population at large and the monarchy. In addition, Denmark had a long history of an ideology that combined Christian humanism and democratic nationalism, and a strong emphasis on individual responsibility and a moral commitment to the community, all of this deeply ingrained in the educational system.

There were no severe splits in Danish society along class, religious, racial, or other minority lines, protecting the maintenance of the national community at large from regression into splits typical of primitive, paranoid group situations.

The Jewish population in Denmark was small—not more than eight thousand people. The Jewish community in Denmark had a long history of integration, equality before the law, and it had been able to integrate newcomers from Eastern Europe successfully in the early part of the century, with a remarkably rapid integration into both the Jewish community itself as well as into the total Danish community.

The democratic and individualistic aspects of political life in Denmark were intimately related to a strong, dominant Lutheran Reformed church, perhaps best expressed by the theologian Hal Koch, the leader of the Union of Danish Youth during the forties. Hal Koch made an ongoing effort, during the German occupation, to stress the need for the entire nation to combine politization, individual and collective responsibility, knowledge of all the facts, and negotiation with the Nazis, as long as that was possible. Thus, in terms of leadership as well as history, the conditions of Danish society were ideal.

Regarding the leadership of Denmark between 1940 and 1943, that is, after the Nazi occupation and before the rescue of the Jews, the history of personal courage on the part of King Christian X was remarkable. The story that he said he would wear the yellow star and, thereby prevented the Germans from imposing the yellow star on the Jewish population at large, may have been apocryphal, but the truth is that the king was an extremely courageous man who maintained openly and publicly his alliance with the Jewish community during the German occupation, and who steadily protested against the German efforts to reduce its civil liberties.

After the German occupation, the Danish political parties formed a council, the famous Council of Nine, which maintained liaison between parliament and the monarchy and permitted the government to negotiate with the Germans on a flexible basis, while yet maintaining contact with the people, whose anti-German and anti-Nazi attitudes provided strength to the government.

In contrast to other countries, there was no betrayal from the top. There was a strong alliance between governors and governed: it was clear to both that they had different responsibilities and had to assume different public postures.

Finally, the leaders of the Danish Resistance and the leaders of the Union of Danish Youth were all willing to wait; they were willing to organize themselves but not involve the nonunderground Danish population until the appropriate moment came—when the Germans reneged on all previous understandings with the government. When it became clear that, first of all, the king was imprisoned during the state of emergency, and that therefore the legal government had ceased to function (except the chief of the administrative heads of the ministries who, of course, no longer had the political basis of power or the independent authority of the king), the Danish Resistance appealed to the general population. Then, in the course of a few weeks, without any public statement or proclamation, the authority of the Resistance increased, and the spontaneous organization of the Danish people to rescue the Jews went into effect.

And, finally, of course, there was the international situation, the Germans' trying to preserve a semblance of normality in their relations with the Danes, their enormous dependence on Danish agricultural products, and the decentralized nature of Danish agricultural production, so that mass resistance would immediately mean a decrease of all exports to Germany. These circumstances motivated at least von Ribbentrop and the German foreign ministry to proceed with care, while, on the other hand, rivalries between the German army, the foreign ministry, and Himmler presented the Danes with contradictory forces operating upon them, and illustrated both the totalitarian and also the chaotic nature of the German administrative system.

I think that two important leaders in all these developments were the German ministers and plenipotentiaries of that time, von Renthe-Fink and Best. Von Renthe-Fink, a relatively non-anti-Semitic Nazi, had recommended, until early 1943, that the Jews be left alone because the Danes would see any movement against Danish Jews as an infringement of their own autonomy and of their political and national rights (which had been formally granted by the Germans). Von Renthe-Fink was finally recalled and replaced by Best, a typical Nazi but not particularly anti-Semitic.

Best was an opportunist who, in order to maintain things smoothly in Denmark, first tried to protect the Jews. However, when he thought the German army was about to assume direct control of the government of Denmark, he tried to maintain his own power with the support of Himmler.

In order to strengthen his political position vis-à-vis Berlin, Best recommended that all Danish Jews be rounded up and deported. Although he denied this later at Nuremberg, the evidence seems to be pretty clear that Best himself triggered that fateful first week of October 1943. After realizing that the entire Danish nation was rising to rescue the Jews, he attempted, at the last moment, a compromise by assuring the Danes that four thousand Danish recruits who had been interned when the Germans entered Copenhagen would be released, and that only the Jews would be deported. Best never understood that this offer would incense and enrage the Danes and reinforce their sense of community and mutual responsibility.

A democratic society with few internal splits with a humanistic ideology rooted in a sense of personal responsibility rather than in messianic generalities, with a sufficient absence of xenophobia and with requisite leadership, permits the activation and expression of personal courage, and the avoidance of both the syndrome of the "innocent bystander" and the corruption of the entire social system.

There is courage in large groups, there is courage in hordes and mobs who storm and burn; but it is not moral courage. There is a moral courage of individuals who are willing to alienate themselves from societies that have fallen prey to paranoid and narcissistic ideologies, but there is also a courage of the individual supported in his moral convictions by the surrounding community which can facilitate a daring, idealistic human response to dangerous threats to the values and human rights of that society.

I realize that the application of a theory of group psychology to an event such as occurred in Denmark in 1943, if correct, may seem to reduce the importance of individual acts of courage and heroism. On the other hand, the absence of explanatory theories may lead us to the hope for other such glorious moments in history as the Danish rescue of the Jews, and to abandon the search for the human and social conditions that may foster such magnificent examples of human fortitude.

Whether or not this analysis of some factors that contributed to the heroic Danish rescue of the Danish Jewish community is accurate, the very fact of Danish individual and collective courage stands out as a unique historical event. Regardless of our explanations for this high point of human history, the Danes deserve our eternal gratitude.

NOTES

1. Or "hordees": see Kernberg, *Internal World and External Reality* (New York: Aronson, 1980).
2. Bion, *Experience in Groups* (New York: Basic Books, 1961).
3. Rice, *Learning for Leadership* (London: Tavistock Publications, 1965).
4. Turquet, "Threats to Identity in the Large Group," in *The Large Group: Dynamics and Therapy*, edited by L. Kreegar (London: Constable, 1975).
5. Anzieu, *The Group and the Unconscious* (London: Routledge and Kegan Paul, 1984).
6. Chasseguet-Smirgel, *The Ego Ideal* (New York: W. W. Norton, 1985).

12.

OBSERVATIONS ON THE DANISH RESCUE

Arthur A. Cohen

In the Danish rescue of the Jews, we are dealing with the issue of moral choice under stress—particularly moral choice as exercised by a cohesive, well-defined, self-clarified people functioning under conditions of excellent democratic and parliamentary sponsorship, led by a benign, wise, and judicious king, bonded by a tradition of Christian sanity—which in these times may well be considered the alternative to Erasmian humanism (were it not for the fact that Erasmus was anti-Jewish). In effect, however, Danish sanity was Danish humanism.

The Jewish community of Denmark had the advantage of being small, integrated, and not particularly distinguished, notable, or public. It produced the occasional figure during the nineteenth-century cultural and literary awakening who proved useful, although Georg Brandes—an early exponent of Strindberg and partisan of Nietzsche—was not a particularly self-aware Jew nor particularly public in the espousal of any significant nineteenth-century Jewish cause.

When I reflect on the situation of so many small Jewish communities in the European diaspora, I often think of Browning's poem *Caliban on Setebos:* communities so small and compact that the diabolic Caliban cannot find them. The Jews of Denmark were well-integrated into Danish society and did not constitute a threat—real or imagined—to the established order.

However, it must be said that for the Danes the rescue of the Jews was an act of resistance, an act of resistance which would have been exercised had Danish society boasted 7,200 blacks or Latinos instead of 7,200 Jews. The Danes would have saved *any* threatened minority. They happened to save Jews. Saving Jews was an act of resistance to the Nazis and hence the alacrity, canniness, ingenuity of organization with which they pursued the saving.

The Jews were the accidental legatees of a spirit of national coherence, a spirit of national self-expression which would accept no humiliation from the Germans as the Danes had been forced to accept earlier, in the nineteenth century, in the border war between Denmark and Germany which Denmark lost.

We thus have a tradition in Danish history of conflict with Germany. We have a tradition of national pride and a tradition of refusal to be humiliated. And finally, we have the accidental *tertium quid*—the small Jewish community of Denmark that became the occasion for a rallying of self-esteem under stress, of pride in exigency. It seems therefore that we may have a reverse process at work; while we praise the Danes for rescuing us, we also praise them for upholding their pride before another threatening humiliation. If they had failed to meet the challenge, their humiliation would have been great for it would have meant that the Danes were not united, that they could no longer uphold that unity of Christian humanism and Danish nationalism which had been their historic strength.

Professor Pelikan described a tradition of folk education (considerably different, I should note, from the Volkish doctrine that functioned in German nationalism through the nineteenth and early twentieth centuries—a Volkish nationalism that led clearly and directly to the National Socialists but produced precisely the opposite effect in Denmark with Grundtvig's formation of a national movement of popular education in values that stressed communal rather than individual initiatives and ethnic diversity rather than ethnic unity and consequent exclusion of minorities.

Danish society valued unity—in which diversity was acknowledged; unity laid the groundwork of order and cohesion, civic duty and civic virtue, moral responsibility and clarity of self-understanding.

The rescue of the Jews was a normal consequence of Danish civic virtue; the Jews were the accidental beneficiaries of a homogeneous, clear, and well-ordered society.

Professor Pelikan, in his attempt to cut behind the distinction of Christian doctrine and Jewish apartness, makes the critical observation of the grounding of popular Christian theology in Denmark. The imperatives of biblical faith were described by Grundtvig as always leading into community, into public action, into the expression of group behavior rather than away from these toward radical individualism, radical social narcissism, personal gratification, and personal fulfillment despite the demands raised by community.

Clearly we can move beyond the social-psychological description of the Danish community or the behavior of groups under stress, beyond the historical characterization of Danish society, beyond the description of the political cohesiveness of Danish culture during the early twentieth century toward raising questions which remain, I believe, still unasked today: namely, the nature of moral courage.

Plato spoke of courage in the *Protagoras,* arguing that very often what passes as courage is really stupidity and folly. However, even here, Plato baited the hook of his unconventional diminishment of courage by suggesting something else about the moral life. His concern was to strip from courage all sentimentality and unrealism. Plato's covert intention was to eliminate the rash and the foolhardy from the performance of courage, moral dumbness from the sphere of moral heroism. Many human beings are capable of gratuitous acts of heroism under stress—breaking up fights, entering the burning house to rescue the trapped, jumping into the water to save the drowning. Such acts are clearly acts of folly and stupidity and yet, nonetheless such acts are successful even if one's life has been risked. It cannot be forgotten then when speaking of the Danish rescue of the Jews that the Danes risked their lives. They acted foolishly, but bravely, stupidly but with extreme heroism.

Confronting then the phenomenon of human beings willing to risk their lives, we return to the original mystery that, despite all our understanding of the moral sources of Danish heroism, all our interpretation of the humanistic vectors of Danish nationalism, there has to be in all human endeavors a courage of character that faces up, that recognizes that here—in the face of threat and violence—human beings were tested and passed, that they were given the opportunity of justifying their presence as human beings upon this earth and they were victorious.

For most of us, the conduct of life is serving pleasure and serving need, but many of us enter life and leave it without ever being challenged to any ultimate decision. Most of us escape this world without ever having had to put ourselves on the line.

Putting ourselves on the line isn't recommended. It isn't something we should seek. For thinkers like Plato who regard rash courage as stupidity, it remains an open question whether putting ourselves on the line for others is ever a wise and indicated move. For me, it is always the wise alternative *in extremis*—when not only single lives are saved but notice is given to the callous and indifferent that saving lives is a religious duty.

EPILOGUE

13.

EXPLAINING THE RESCUE OF THE DANISH JEWS

LEO GOLDBERGER

Civilization means, above all, an unwillingness to inflict unnecessary pain. Within the ambit of that definition, those of us who heedlessly accept the commands of authority cannot yet claim to be civilized men.

—Harold J. Laski (1929)

AMONG THE THEMES one consistently finds in the Danish literature on the remarkable rescue of the Jews in 1943, perhaps the most salient is the tone with which the story is told, especially by the rescuers themselves. The tone is one of modesty. Whether one reads the formal historical accounts or the more anecdotal ones, the insistence on shrugging off the attribution of heroism or special courage, unusual level of morality or altruism, is unmistakably present. The Danes point out that the special set of circumstances that prevailed in their country during the war makes comparisons with other countries inappropriate. And they characteristically assert that, under the given circumstances, they could not possibly have behaved in any other way (and live with their consciences). Their determination to help their fellow human being, whatever his or her religious bent or origin, in the hour of impending disaster—the senseless, brutal persecution of innocent men, women, and children—was the most natural impulse. It required little, if any, hesitation or deliberation.[1] It was, indeed, *spontaneous*—a psychological feature of the act which adds to its remarkable and awe-inspiring nature. Now to say that an act is spontaneous does not mean that it is created *de novo,* without prior determinants—historical, socio-cultural, political, familial, developmental, intra and interpersonal, situational, and so on. In the case of the Danish rescue the determinants were, as we have seen in the foregoing pages, not only multiple and interconnected, but also varied in terms of conceptual level and relative distance from the act to be explained.

Professor Hæstrup, undoubtedly the leading Danish historian of the occupation years, has here (chapter 2) and elsewhere (e.g. *Til Landets Bedste* and *Besættelsen 1940–45*) provided us with perhaps the most authoritative deliniation of the historical, political and intergroup determinants. In addition, it should be noted that the Israeli political scientist Dr. Leni Yahil, has provided us with her highly readable book *The Rescue of Danish Jewery,* which fortunately is available in English and which is focused entirely on this subject. She offers the reader a vast array of documentary evidence and source material in support of her overriding thesis that the rescue of the Jews may be viewed as having been a test of the resilience of Danish democracy at a critical juncture in Denmark's history. Whether one accepts her conceptual framework or not—and it does have its detractors, especially among some Danish critics who find it dubious and a bit too lofty in its level of abstraction and among some Danish Jews who find her depiction of the Jewish leadership of their community a bit askew—the factual material in her book is sufficiently detailed to allow the reader alternative interpretive explanations. She, like Professor Hæstrup, suggests a number of broadly conceived factors—five in all, in Dr. Yahil's case—which she feels must be acknowledged as necessary, though undoubtedly not fully sufficient, before one can begin to understand the remarkable feat of the mass rescue. For the purpose of providing the reader of this volume a brief overview of the rescue and its contextual background, I shall list her five factors and follow each with a brief discussion and a personal comment or two, in an attempt to explicate some of the subordinate aspects of each. I will present the ideas rather discursively, in broad strokes, with no pretense of primary scholarship. In fact, most of the ideas here may be found scattered thoughout the pages of Professor Hæstrup, Dr. Yahil, and others who will be cited.

1. "THE SMALL NUMBER OF JEWS IN DENMARK"

Quite obviously it is easier to save a small rather than a large number of people, no matter what the context. But the fact of there having been relatively few Jews in Denmark—less than eight thousand in a population of four and a half million—takes on added significance when one considers a related point, namely the relative absence, historically, of anti-Semitism in Denmark.[2] As Bent Melchior's article (chapter 3) details, there may have been rifts between the old Jewish families, already fully integrated into Danish society, and the Russian immigrant Jews who arrived after the turn of the century, but as an aggregate both groups were essentially accepted by the Danish community at large. And as is true for any small minority, the pressure to fit in, to become integrated with and to find acceptance by the majority group (especially one as homogeneous as the Danish), at least in terms of the language, customs, mode of dress, and other *external* aspects, was undoubtedly enormous (cf. Blum, Rohde,). Yet, as Melchior points out, Jews did survive as a religous entity (culturally, to a lesser extent) in the face of considerable pressure.

Parenthetically, among the external pressures were those of Danish missionary groups, who in their own well-meaning Christian way strove to convert Jews and bring them salvation. By their own account, these efforts were not particularly successful in Denmark (cf. Sandbæk and Rald, pp. 100–13). It is interesting to note further that for some of the rescurers, many of whom were indeed drawn from the ranks of the clergy or were from rural areas where fundamental Evangelist teachings held sway, theological considerations played not an insignificant *positive* role in their position on the Jews and on anti-Semitism (cf. Fulgsang-Damgaard's pastoral letter, p. 7 in this volume and also his chapter in Refslund and Schmidt; Sandbæk and Rald; Borchsenius; Bertelsen; and Tortzen, among others.) Poul Borchsenius, the so-called fighting priest whose underground activities required his own escape to Sweden in 1943, made a telling point by divorcing himself from the dominant view of the clergy of that period and by voicing his belief that there·is more than one road to salvation—that Christians have one road and the Jews another.[3] In this connection, Professor Pelikan's article (chapter 10) adds some valuable clarification for us by pointing to the special blend of nationalism, humanism, and Lutheranism that was due to Grundtvig's influence on the Danish state church.

2. "THE SPECIAL POLITICAL CONDITIONS PREVAILING IN THE MODEL PROTECTORATE OF THE GERMANS"

Professor Hæstrup's overview in this volume affords a precise account of the special nature of the governmental relations between Denmark and the Germans. Of paramount significance is the Danish insistence on keeping absolute control of its own domestic affairs, including as a high order of priority, the continued enjoyment of full civil rights for all its citizens, including Jews. (Some two hundred Danish Communists, as Professor Hæstrup points out, did not fare too well on this score.) As far as the Danish authorities were concered there was "no Jewish problem" for the Germans to be concerned with. But, more than that, it was none of their business, Danes felt, for it was a domestic issue. The carefully defined and minutely monitored agreement of accommodation entered into by the Danes (through its popularly elected government, not the Quisling type that took over Norway) had certain important consequences. For instance, Jewish life continued essentially undisturbed; no gradual divestiture of rights was instituted; no requirement that Jews be identified by wearing the yellow Star of David ever was broached with the king or any government official (see Thaulow, Barfoed). In brief, the so-called Nuremberg laws were not implemented in Denmark, at least not until the crisis of autumn 1943.

As a corollary of the official policy of peaceful accommodation, the necessity for massive deployment of Nazi personnel—Gestapo, the SS, and other Nazi security forces—was relatively small, though the band of treacherous, uniformed Danish Nazis and informers amply made up for the shortage and contributed to the general terror among Danish citizens. The military—the *Wehrmacht*—was there in great strength, but not the more brutal, Jew-baiting, Nazi party. The significance of this fact comes to the fore in various ways. It helps to account, for example, for the dismal failure, on purely tactical grounds, of the 1–2 October roundup of the Jews, which was primarily a Nazi effort with secondary assistance by *Wehrmacht* soldiers who often closed their eyes and allowed Jews to slip away. But perhaps even more importantly, the disparity in number, as well as the ambiguity of authority and personal rivalry among the various components of power in the convoluted German hierarchy, may have been responsible for Dr. Best's own peculiarly ambivalent behavior and half-hearted approach to the roundup. The much-heralded warning by Best's confidant, G. F. Duckwitz, after Best himself initiated the Jewish action via a crucial telegram on 8 September (which despite valiant efforts could not be intercepted before it was read by Hitler himself and then it was too late), was but the tip of this complicated internal strife. The discord among the Germans in charge of Denmark included a clash of views and attitudes toward Hitler and his racial policies. The true nature of Best's motivation in initiating the fateful action against the Jews (despite his and his associates' forecast of the uproar it was likely to cause among the Danes) remains a mystery to this day. His own claim—that he knew the order for the action from Berlin was forthcoming and that by proposing it himself he insured its failure—is unconvincing. Dr. Best was an early and high-ranking member of the SS, a legalistic and administrative bureaucrat, he showed a masterful penchant for double dealing, if not for psychopathic deceit.[4] He had arrived on the scene in late 1942 presumably to "toughen up" the German presence in Denmark after the departure of the previous chief representative of Germany, von Renthe-Fink, who unlike Best was a career diplomat and not especially nazified. After the end of the war, to the chagrin of many, Werner Best was released after serving only half of the twelve-year sentence imposed by the Danish courts. Since then, he has been practicing law in the Rhineland, apparently helping other Nazis with their defense (see Brovst).

3. "THE GEOGRAPHIC PROXIMITY OF SWEDEN"

To appreciate fully the importance of geography in the fate of the Danish Jews the reader should keep in mind that, despite the proximity of Sweden (just a few miles across the sound in some places), illegal passage across was considered almost impossible. Not only were there the German-monitored Danish exit controls and an efficient coast guard to contend with, but also Sweden's "neutrality." There was, thus, no guarantee of a Swedish welcome should a boatload of refugees arrive—at least not before the critical juncture in 1943, when Swedish foreign policy finally turned around from a pro-German to a more pro-Allies neutrality. A hectic series of diplomatic maneuvers—involving Swedes and Germans, others involving Danes and Swedes at the highest levels of diplomacy and government—as well as through appeals by prominent private citizens, including a personal visit with the Swedish king by Niels Bohr who himself had escaped to Sweden only a few days before the roundup, finally led the Swedish governement on 1 October to announce, publicly, its offer of sanctuary to the endangered Danish Jews. Only with this move, could the mass exodus from Denmark to Sweden even be contemplated as a reality by those who were trying, by hook or by crook, to figure out some way to help their Jewish compatriots.

The Swedish move also spelled the beginning of that country's magnificent humanitarian contributions, which exceeded all expectations, and for which it can be justly proud. The courageous efforts by Raoul Wallenberg on behalf of the Hungarian Jews in 1944 is but one case in point (see Lester).

4. "THE DATE OF THE PERSECUTIONS—AUTUMN 1943—AFTER THE GERMAN DEFEAT OF EL ALAMEIN AND STALINGRAD HAD MARKED THE TURNING POINT OF THE WAR"

The significance of timing as a factor is weighty, but it needs some elaboration beyond pointing out that autumn of 1943 was the turning point in the war. That was of course a significant though distant factor. What needs to be added is the singular importance of the activities of the Danish resistance movement especially in the autumn of 1943. (In fact, in my view, Dr. Yahil might well have listed it separately as a major determinant in its own right.)

By early 1943, the Danish resistance movement, though small in size, initially only some three to four thousand (which, ironically was no more than the total number of Danish Nazis), not only had inflicted damage upon the Germans physically and psychologically, but had boosted the morale of the Danish people as a whole.[5] Through its underground, the anonymous Freedom Council formally established on 16 September 1943, in a secret hideout in Copenhagen, constituted Denmark's *de facto* leadership. The council consisted of mostly nonpoliticians, each representing a different underground faction, including the influential illegal press (see Lefevre). The resistance movement had an incalculable effect in the international arena, readily earning Denmark its membership in the United Nations as an allied nation—despite the first few years of Danish-German accommodation by the professional politicians. Its widely heralded performance of bravery and courage, its cunningly creative and frequently humorous twitting of the Germans, which characterized its virile *modus operandi,* its ultimate sacrifices—the many brave and energetic lives lost in the fight for freedom and the many scarring experiences of German imprisonment—shall be forever honored and remembered.

The resistance movement gave the Danes hope and a sense of pride in spite of widespread ambivalence, uneasiness, and opposition by the official government). It also provided role models for those who were quite suddenly and unexpectedly drawn into their first illegal activity: the novel work of hiding and helping their Jewish friends, neighbors, and compatriots. These helpers were drawn from all sectors of Danish life and were by and large *not* members of the active underground. And rightly so, for members of the underground were constantly at risk of capture themselves. Nevertheless, the resistance movement was behind the Jewish rescue all the way, but typically "behind the scene." Members of the resistance were the resourceful experts on such matters as hiding places, fund raising, land and sea transportation, intelligence gathering, etc. It should be underscored that the "amateurs," those suddenly drawn into the month-long rescue effort which succeeded in getting almost all the Jews saved, quickly became quite adept at the work; many continued in the active resistance until the war's end. Perhaps more significantly, the resistance movement gained popular acceptance, constituting quite an important turning point in the eyes of most students of the period.

The timing of the action against the Jews, it should be recalled, came in the wake of *the* most critical point: the political crisis of 29 August. The crisis had come in the aftermath of increased sabotage, unrest, and general strikes in a number of towns and cities across the land and which Danish authorities and Danish police were unable to squelch on their own. In a sense, it may be concluded that the German "overreaction" to this failure on the part of the Danish authorities—that is, the brutal German reprisals, proposed encroachments on the initial agreement of peaceable cooperation, and, finally, the Jewish persecution—led fairly directly to the desired aim of the resistance movement: to have a popular revolt against the oppressor.

Following 29 August, the Danes were ready for some sort of action. Denmark was now a country without a real government. It was a country which had its symbolic father figure, beloved old King Christian X, under German guard. It was a country with its army stripped, demobilized, and sequestered in detention camps. Now add the strain of a "state of emergency"—curfew laws, prohibitions, and threats of all kinds, not to mention the deliberate and increased display of massive military and police force, tanks, machine guns in readiness, hundreds of uniformed soldiers, *Wehrmacht* and SS—against the chronic background of food rationing, unexpected sabotage bombings, allied air raids, fires, the piercing sound of sirens and distant explosions, liquidations, and almost nightly hours-long stays in musty underground shelters, and you have the approximate picture. For a peace-loving, "neutral" country, with its famous facade of good humor, it was getting rough—and on a very personal level—with frustrated rage widespread, edging toward retaliatory, if not explosive release.

In the absence of a duly constituted Danish authority, the internalized restraints that ordinarily governed the behavior of the average, law-abiding Dane were drastically diminished. Most people who had, up to this point, stuck to their comfortable routine and who at most might have engaged in furtive reading of one of the many illegal papers (which urged widespread anti-German action), listening to the BBC, enjoying the release afforded by anti-German jokes, or partaking of other harmless bravado behavior, were now ready to act. These were individuals, constituting the majority of Danes, who had shied away from "illegal acts," lest they violate the law and order so insistently called for by their king and government (see Pedersen, Frisch et. al.). Yet, finally, after months of reflection and *sub rosa* debate dividing family members and friends, they were more than ready to act!

When the rumor of a persecution of Jews arose and grew in force, it signified the proverbial last straw. This was finally, and quite suddenly, to be *the* direct, close-to-home confrontation with the senseless, brutally inhuman and totally unfathomable Nazi mentality and behavior. For most people, it was their first encounter with its reality. The response by the Danes was immediate, spontaneous, and from the heart. They were magnificent! They *cared*. They *empathized*. They *helped*. They put themselves on the line. They were, thereby, quite unintentionally and unwittingly afforded an effective, meaningful, and long-to-be remembered outlet for their pent-up energy and emotions, not the least among which was the desire to get back at those damned Germans!

The above bit of psychologizing is, unlike good historical scholarship, clearly more speculative although it *is* based on at least a sampling of primary source material (Meyer, Kiær, Gersfelt, Svendstorp, Welner, and Tortzen, among others), interviews, and personal experience. Be that as it may, I want to emphasize that in no way is this formulation intended to detract from the quality of the moral choice embedded in the final outcome—the wonderfully spontaneous and natural act of rescue! It is only to suggest the complexity of human behavior and its multilayered, motivational determinants. Altruistic behavior may, indeed, have among its codeterminants such motives as adventure seeking and, in some rarer instances perhaps, even a profit motive.[6]

To explicate and grasp fully the kind of spontaneous, grassroots movement that led to the rescue—which, at a minimum, involved an upsurge of concern, neighborliness and group solidarity, hospitality, and financial generosity, and at a maximum entailed all kinds of life-threatening risks for the rescuers—is not a simple proposition. It not only requires knowledge derived from social and psychological realms to explain individual and group behavior under conditions of disaster and stress (see Goldberger and Breznitz), but cross-culturally it also calls for a grasp of national-character structure—risky ethnographic turf perhaps better avoided except in a most cautiously qualified way.

5. "The special character and moral stature of the Danish people and their love of democracy and freedom"

With this, Dr. Yahil's final category, she strives to capture a set of determinants that she accords a pivotal role, superordinate to all the others. Though it is difficult to assess objectively, my reading of Danish history and firsthand familiarity with its culture makes me concur wholeheartedly with Dr. Yahil's judgment of its importance. Even a superficial knowledge of Danish history yields up the striking impression of an array of sociopolitical milestones which in their aggregate suggest that Danes champion freedom, independence, and, above all, democracy. It is surely not accidental that Denmark was ahead of the times when it gave its peasants their freedom, when it outlawed slave trading in the Danish West Indies, when it established its constitutional monarchy or, indeed, when it accorded full civil rights to its Jewish settlers. Nor is Denmark's international reputation for progressive social welfare accidental, not to mention its contemporary concern for political refugees, its assistance to third-world countries, and its antinuclear policies.

Even the collective shame that readily reveals itself in Danish postwar polemics at having "buckled under" on 9 April 1940 may be viewed as evidence for Dr. Yahil's thesis. Despite the David-and-Goliath odds that the government and the king perceived, for a people whose love of freedom and independence was paramount, it was an intolerable compromise. Love of freedom took second place, at least temporarily, to the political pragmatics of saving lives and property—and to maintaining neutrality.

But it hardly needs affirming here, in a volume paying tribute to the Danes, that the Danes more than compensated for this initial stance. In fact from the very beginning of the occupation, the Danes demonstrated through their solidarity, revival of national and spiritual fellowship with its thousand-year-old roots, and their detached, cold-shoulder approach to the Germans that they were emotionally in opposition. And no sooner had the reins of leadership passed on to others than the Danes were off and running, "doing their thing." It is, indeed, to their credit that after the war was over the Danes went through an excruciating amount of soul-searching and official enquiry, examining all aspects of their behavior during the occupation. If self-examination be a national-character trait of the Danes, then it surely speaks for a high level of moral development. Quite parenthetically, how is one to pass judgment on whether the government's stand on 9 April 1940 was wise or not? The Danish historian and Social-Democrat, Hartvig Frisch (vol. 3, p. 356), in his discussion of this issue, resolves it by citing an apt passage from Plato's political dialogues, in which soberness is contrasted with bravery. It is, says Socrates, a question of finding an optimal balance between these two inherently inimical tendencies among citizens in a society. It would seem that Denmark achieved just that optimal mix. Its sober government and its brave resistance each contributed to the ultimate welfare of the society.

In writing about Denmark's refusal to forsake its Jewish population, Thomas Merton raised the frequently asked question: "Why did a course of action which worked so simply and so well in Denmark not occur to all the other so-called Christian nations of the West just as simply and just as spontaneously?" The answer he offered deserves repetition as it contains a profound and movingly appropriate observation which Danish modesty and avoidance of lofty generalizations may make it difficult for the Danes to voice themeselves:

> Obviously there is no simple answer. It does not even necessarily follow that the Danes are men of greater faith or deeper piety than other western Europeans. But perhaps it is true that these people had been less perverted and secularized by the emptiness and cynicism, the thoughtlessness, the crude egoism and the rank amorality which has become characteristic of our world, even where we still see an apparent surface of Christianity. It is not so much that the

Danes were Christians, as they were *human*. How many others were even that?

The Danes were able to do what they did because they were able to make decisions that were based on clear convictions about which they all agreed and which were in accord with the inner truth of man's own rational nature, as well as in accordance with the fundamental law of God in the Old Testament as well as in the Gospel: thou shalt love thy neighbor as thyself. The Danes were able to resist the cruel stupidity of Nazi anti-Semitism because this fundamental truth was *important* to them. And because they were willing, in unanimous and concerted action to stake their lives on this truth. In a word, *such action becomes possible where fundamental truths are taken seriously*. (Merton, p. 167).

NOTES

1. It most certainly did not require the kind of *cognitive* (meaning essentially conscious) "decision-making process" that some of our more "scientistic", model-building psychologists would posit.

2. Though there may be a general correlation between the majority-minority ratio and anti-Semitism, this is by no means a causal one; anti-Semitism is essentially irrational, and may flair up or remain dormant as a function of the general economic-political situation at a given time.

3. Taped interview with Poul Borchsenius conducted by the late Norma Greensteen for the New York radio station WEVD. This taped interview, along with those of other Danish rescuers and underground figures (Aage Bertelsen, Richard Ege, Mogens Fog) was provided by Professor Samuel Abrahamsen of Brooklyn College.

4. Before his foreign ministry assignment under Ribbentrop, Best had worked for Himmler and Gestapo chief Heydrich.

5. Before the resistance movement could manufacture its own sorely needed arms and explosives, they were parachuted down by the English; the free "Danish Council" in London, already formed by September 1940, served as sabotage and training coordinator.

6. This is of course a matter of definition. There is wide disagreement of how to define the preconditions for altruistic behavior, whether to allow for motives other than helping others purely "out of the goodness of one's heart," with no apparent social or personal gain in the offing, or whether, as I do, to allow for additional, though peripheral, conscious or unconscious motives. (For an extensive treatment of this and other relevant issues see Bar-Tal, Berkowitz, Krebs, Macaulay & Berkowitz, and Staub).

REFERENCES

Barfoed, O. *Jødestjernen kom aldrig til Danmark.* Copenhagen: Politikens Kronik, 1 October 1983.

Bar-Tal, D. *Prosocial Behavior.* New York: Halsted Press, 1976.

Berkowitz, L. (ed.) *Advances in Experimental and Social Psychology,* vol. 6. New York: Academic Press, 1972.

Bertelsen, Aa. *Oktober 43: Oplevelser tilstande under Jødeforfølgelsen i Danmark.* Aarhus: Jydsk Centraltrykkeris Forlag, 1952.

Blum, J. *Dansk og/eller jøde.* Copenhagen: Gyldendals Samfundsbibliotek, 1972.

Borchsenius, P. *Kæmp for alt: Billeder fra en dansk Provinsby under Gestapos Søgelys!* Copenhagen: Branner, 1946.

———. *To veje.* Copenhagen: Samlerens Forlag, 1977.

Brovst, B. N. *Jødedeportationen i Danmark og Werner Best.* Copenhagen: ZAC, 1981.

Frisch, H.; Buhl, V.; Hedtoft, H.; & Jensen, E. (eds.) *Danmark besat og befriet,* vols 1, 2, & 3. Copenhagen: Fremad, 1945–48.

Gersfelt, J. *Saadan narrede vi Gestapo.* Copenhagen: Gyldendal, 1945.

Goldberger, L., & Breznitz, S. (eds.) *Handbook of Stress.* New York: Free Press, 1982.

Hæstrup, J. *Til Landets Bedste,* vols 1 & 2. Copenhagen: Gyldendal: 1966, 1971.

———; Kirchhoff, H; Poulsen, H.; & Petersen, H. (eds.) *Besætelsen 1940–45: Politik, Modstand, Befrielse.* Copenhagen: Politikens Forlag, 1979.

Kiær, E. *Med Gestapo i Kølvandet.* Copenhagen: Frimodt, 1945

Krebs, D. L. "Altruism—An Examination of the Concept and a Review of the Literature." *Psychological Bulletin,* 1970, 73: 258–302.

la Cour, V.(ed.) *Danmark under Besættelsen.* Copenhagen: Westermann, 1945–47, vols 1–3.

Laski, H. J. The Dangers of Obedience. *Harpers Monthly Magazine,* June 1929, 159:1–10.

Lefevre, H. *Mændene i' Danmarks Frihedsraad.* Copenhagen: Wilhelm Prior, 1945.

Lester, E. *Wallenberg: The Man in the Iron Web.* Englewood Cliffs, N.J.: Prentice Hall, 1982.

Macaulay, J., & Berkowitz, L. (eds.) *Altruism and Helping Behavior.* New York: Academic Press, 1970.

Merton, T. *The Non-Violent Alternative.* New York: Farrar, Strauss, Giroux, 1971.

Meyer, T. L. *Flugten over Øresund*. Copenhagen: Jespersen og Pios, 1945.

Pedersen, O. *Den Politiske Modstand under Besættelsen*. Copenhagen: Gyldendal, 1946.

Refslund, C., & Schmidt, M. *Fem Aar: Intryk og Oplevelser*. Copenhagen: Hagerups, 1946.

Rohde, Ina. *Da jeg blev Jøde i Danmark*. Copenhagen: C. A. Reitzel, 1982.

Sandbæk, H., & Rald, N. J. (eds.) *Den Danske Kirke under Besættelsen*. Copenhagen: H. Hirschsprung, 1945.

Staub, E. *Positive Social Behavior and Morality*, vols. 1 & 2. New York: Academic Press, 1978–79.

Svendstorp, A. (ed.) *Den hvide Brigade: Danske Lægers Modstand*. Copenhagen: Carl Allers, 1946.

Thaulow, T. *Konge og Folk gennem Brændingen 1937–1945*. Copenhagen: H. Hagerup, 1945.

Tortzen, C. *Gilleleje October 1943*. Copenhagen: Fremad. 1970.

Yahil, L. *The Rescue of Danish Jewry: Test of a Democracy*. Philadelphia: Jewish Publication Society, 1969.

Welner, P. *Krigen mod Jøderne*. Copenhagen: R. Wangel, 1946.

———. *Ved Øresunds Bredder*. Copenhagen: Thaning & Appel, 1953.

The defeated and demoralized Germans were routed—on foot. The Danish freedom fighters and brigade members confiscated the Germans' weapons, luxury cars, and thousands of bicycles that had been stolen from Danes. Departing, too, were more than two hundred thousand German civilians who had taken refuge in Denmark.

Fifth of May 1945: the war has ended and jubilation is everywhere. Soon after the fifth the Allied troops—primarily British, but American and Russian as well—arrived. There were endless festivities, music, and dancing as well as the tension of hunting down informers, collaborators, and Nazis in flight. One hundred seventy were sentenced to death.

OPPOSITE

Field Marshal Montgomery receives a hero's welcome down Strøget, Copenhagen's famous promenade. A few days earlier, on 9 May, King Christian was similary greeted by enthusiastic crowds as he and the queen rode in an open car to open the first free parliament since the war.

BIBLIOGRAPHY

BOOKS

(This is a general list of some of the relevant literature available in English.)

Adler, H. G. "Danish Jewry Under German Occupation." The Wiener Library Bulletin, vol. 9, 1955.

Arneson, Ben A. *The Democratic Monarchies of Scandinavia.* New York: van Norstrand, 1949.

Arnold, Elliot. *A Night of Watching.* New York: Scribner, 1967.

Bamberger, Ib Nathan. *The Viking Jews: A History of the Jews of Denmark.* New York: Shengold, 1983.

Barfod, Jørgen H. *The Holocaust Failed in Denmark.* Copenhagen: Frihedsmuseets Venners, 1985.

Bauer, Yehuda. *A History of the Holocaust.* New York: Franklin Watts, 1982.

Benchley, Nathaniel. *Bright Candles.* New York: Harper and Row, 1974.

Bertelsen, Aage. *October 43.* New York: Putnam, 1954.

Flender, Harold. *Rescue in Denmark.* New York: Simon & Schuster, 1963; Holocaust Library, 1980.

Friedman, Philip. *Their Brothers' Keepers: The Christian Heroes and Heroines Who Helped the Oppressed Escape the Nazi Terror.* New York: Crown, 1957; Holocaust Library, 1978.

Gilbert, Martin. *The Holocaust: The History of the Jews of Europe During the Second World War.* New York: Holt, Rinehart and Winston, 1985.

Gutman, Yisrael, and Zuroff, Ephraim. "Rescue Attempts During the Holocaust": in *Proceedings of the Second Yad Vashem International Historical Conference, April 1974.* Jerusalem: Vad Vashem, 1977.

Hæstrup, Jørgen. *The Secret Alliance,* 3 vols. New York: New York University Press, 1985.

———. *Passage to Palestine: Young Jews in Denmark 1932–1945*. Odense: Odense University Press, 1983.

Hansen, Poul. *Contemporary Danish Politicians*. Copenhagen: Det Danske Selskab, 1949.

Hilberg, Raul. *The Destruction of the European Jews*. Chicago: Quadrangle, 1961; rev. ed., New York: Holmes and Meier, 1985.

Lampe, David. *The Danish Resistance*. New York: Ballantine, 1960.

Lauwerys, J. A. (ed.) *Scandinavian Democracy*. Copenhagen: Det Danske Selskab, 1958.

Lund, Jens. "The Legend of the King and the Star." *Indiana Folklore*, vol. 8, No. 1–2, 1975.

Melchior, Marcus. *A Rabbi Remembers*. New York: Lyle Stuart, 1968.

Muffs, Judith Herschlag, and Klein, Dennis B. (eds.) *The Holocaust in Books and Films: A Selected, Annotated List*. New York. Intern. Center for Holocaust Studies, Anti-Defamation League of B'nai B'rith.

Menze, Ernest (ed.) *Five Years: The Occupation of Denmark in Pictures*. Malmö, Sweden: A. B. Allheim, 1946.

Muus, Flemming. *The Spark and the Flame*. London: Museum Press, 1957.

Nissen, Henrik S. (ed.) *Scandinavia During the Second World War*. Minneapolis: The University of Minnesota Press, 1983.

Outze, Børge (ed.) *Denmark During the German Occupation*. Copenhagen: Scandinavia Publishing Co., 1946.

Petrow, Richard. *The Bitter Years: The Invasion of Denmark and Norway, April 1940–May 1945*. New York: Morrow, 1974.

Reilly, Robin. *The Sixth Floor*. London: Leslie Frewin, 1969.

Roi, Emilie, *A Different Story: About a Danish Girl in World War Two*. Dallas, Texas.: Rossel Books, 1987.

Rittner, Carol, and Myers, Sondra. (eds.) *The Courage to Care: Rescuers of Jews During the Holocaust*. New York: New York University Press, 1986.

Shirer, William L. *The Challenge of Scandinavia*. Boston: Little, Brown, 1955.

———. *The Rise and Fall of the Third Reich: A History of Nazi Germany*. New York: Simon & Schuster, 1960.

Valentin, Hugo. *Rescue Activities on* Behalf *of Jewish Victims of Nazism in Scandinavia*. New York: Yivo Annual of Jewish Social Science, vol 8, 1953.

Wuorio, Eva-Lis. *To Fight in Silence*. New York: Holt, Rinehart & Winston, 1973.

Yahill, Leni. "Denmark Under the Occupation: A survey of Danish Literature." *The Wiener Library Bulletin,* vol. 16, 1962.

Yahil, Leni. *The Rescue of Danish Jewry: Test of a Democracy*. Philadelphia: Jewish Publication Society, 1969.

FILMS

Act of Faith

Originally presented on CBS-TV (Harold Flender), it is a first-hand account of how the Danes saved their Jewish countrymen, filmed in Denmark. Twenty-eight minutes/black-and-white. Available through Anti-Defamation League of B'nai B'rith, New York.

The Bookseller

Dramatization of an actual incident between a bookseller-resistance leader and a Gestapo captain who loved the banned German author Heinrich Heine. Thirty minutes/black-and-white. Available through National Academy of Adult Jewish Studies, United Synagogues of America, New York.

Denmark '43

An experiment in historical imagination in which a Danish high school teacher guides his students through a dramatic reenactment of the rescue of Jews. Filmed on location in a small fishing village. Twenty-two minutes/16 mm, color. Available through National Center for Jewish Film, Brandeis University.

The Only Way

Set in 1943, this gripping feature movie, produced by a professional Danish film company and outstanding cast, dramatizes the story of the escape of a Jewish family. Eighty-six minutes/16 mm & video cassette, color. Shortened version available for educational purposes through Tribute To the Danes, 1185 Park Avenue, New York.

INDEX